A TASTE OF THE
Mediterranean

A TASTE OF THE
Mediterranean

Classic recipes from
Spain, France, Italy, Greece, and Lebanon

Edited by Diana Vowles

CHARTWELL
BOOKS, INC.

A QUINTET BOOK

Published by Chartwell Books. Inc.
A Division of Book Sales, Inc.
114 Nortfield Avenue,
Edison, New Jersey 08837

This edition produced for sale in the U.S.A.,
its territories and dependencies only.

ISBN 0-7858-0559-1

This book is designed and produced by
Quintet Publishing Limited
6 Blundell Street
London N7 9BH

Creative Director: Richard Dewing
Designer: Bruce Low
Project Editor: Anna Briffa

Typeset in Great Britain by
Central Southern Typesetters, Eastbourne
Manufactured in China by Regent Publishing Services Ltd
Printed in China by Leefung-Asco Printers Ltd

The material in this book was compiled from the following titles:
Portuguese Cooking, The Fresh Pasta Cookbook,
Vegetarian Pasta Cookbook, Lebanese Cooking,
Greek Meze Cooking and *Tapas*

Contents

INTRODUCTION

· · · ·

Mediterranean food has always been a delight, full of tangy, fresh flavors and redolent of bright, hot days and long, warm evenings. Now it's been discovered that it's also the healthiest way of eating, we can also feel virtuous as we tuck in!

The range covered by Mediterranean food is vast, and this book aims to present you with just a selection of characteristic dishes from a variety of countries whose coastlines are lapped by the Mediterranean. The cuisine of some, such as Italy, is already very familiar, and popular, abroad – there can surely be few people who have never sampled pasta and pizza. Other cuisines such as Lebanese and Portuguese are not so well-known but are every bit as delicious.

GREECE

Meze is perhaps the most famous feature of Greek cuisine and, although the spelling may vary, its meaning is always the same. The *meze* is a titbit of food, a small serving of something delicious to accompany a glass of something cool as you sit back and relax in the Mediterranean sunshine, chatting to friends and passers-by.

In Greece, meze is served at every cafe, in every house and on many a street corner. It can be anything from a small nibble of toasted pumpkin seeds to a whole array of tempting salads, dried-bean dishes, dips, tiny kabobs, vegetables – stuffed and unstuffed – and much, much more, creating a mass of colors, tastes and textures, all chosen to complement and enhance each other.

If you are one of those people who finds it difficult to choose from a menu or to decide what to cook for a special occasion, meze is the answer to your prayers. A little bit of everything keeps you satisfied and your guests interested as the myriad dishes flow from the kitchen until you couldn't possibly take any more . . . well, maybe

just one more! Of course, you need not restrict the Greek recipes in this book to the authentic meze table. Any one of them can be added to a menu, prepared for a light lunch, served as an appetizer or a dessert, whenever you feel like adding a taste of Greece to the occasion. You may want to increase the quantities of ingredients if, say, one meze dish is to be served as a main course on its own (remember to allow for extra cooking time, too). That's the wonderful thing about Greek meze cooking – you can always add a little extra of one thing or another if you have a sudden unexpected guest arrive, or you simply want the dish to stretch a little bit further.

Meze cooking exemplifies the Greek way of life – it's relaxed in every aspect. There is no particular way to serve most meze dishes; you simply pick and choose the ones you like best and lay them out for one and all to help themselves. You can offer a selection of vegetarian dishes on their own, or a variety including meat and fish dishes as well. Most of the dishes can be prepared in advance, others can be left to simmer or be reheated just before serving – so whatever the occasion, with Greek meze food you'll be sure to have plenty of time to enjoy its preparation.

LEBANON

Lebanon has played host to invaders, refugees, settlers and merchants since 2000 BC; today it claims to be the only country in the world whose population is composed entirely of minorities, though all call themselves Arabs. These divisions, drawn along religious lines, are reflected in the influences that have united to create Lebanese cuisine.

The large Muslim population is divided almost equally between Sunnis and Shiites, the latter group augmented in the past 20 years by many Palestinian refugees. The very slightly smaller Christian population is dominated by the Maronites, an ancient sect, united to Rome since the thirteenth century. The Maronites, by virtue of their commercial success and historical ties with France, have long been the most educated,

cosmopolitan group in the country, and have actively cultivated the sophistication associated with all things French. The other important minorities include the Druse, a secretive religious sect whose feats of arms are legendary; Orthodox and Catholic Greeks; Armenians and Syrians; and a small community of Jews.

It is the Arabic-Muslim tradition that has ensured the survival of herbed or spiced olive oil and lemon juice as the ubiquitous dressing and marinade; that has confirmed the domination of yogurt over cream (a French contribution); that accounts for the prevalence of lamb-based meat

dishes and the absence of pork; that has developed the range of meze to triumphant heights, and has incorporated a variety of nuts into savory dishes and made them one of the mainstays of sweets, pastries and such rare delicacies as green almond jelly.

It is the French-Maronite influence that has brought wine to the table and vinegar into the kitchen; that has introduced new and succulent vegetables to cultivation and the Syrian truffle into fine Beirut restaurants; that has refined the sometimes aggressive spicing of the East into a subtlety appreciated by Westerners. These two main traditions have historically welcomed the contributions of neighbors and the other ethnic communities: the dates of the Iraqis and the dried fruit dishes of the Jews and Palestinians; the beef dishes and meat stews of the Armenians; the pomegranate seeds and the sumac of the Iranians and Syrians; the pasta of the Italians.

Breakfast is the lightest meal of the day, consisting typically of *labnch* (yogurt cheese) with *khoubz* (Arab bread). Olives, dates, fresh fruits, honey and nuts will also share the table. Country people may eat a bowl of *ful medames* (small brown fava beans), while eggs, fried or hard-cooked, are another alternative.

Lunch, taken between 1 pm and 3 pm, can be the main meal among rural folk, but more usually it is an abbreviated spread of meze with fresh *khoubz*. In Beirut and other large towns, snack bars have proliferated, as they have in Western cities; they are life-savers for the office worker.

Dinner, for most Lebanese, is the main meal of the day, taken with the whole family. Eaten between 8 pm and 11 pm, it consists of a selection of meze – the number and quality of which are dictated by the occasion and the prosperity of the family – grilled meat or poultry (or, on the coast, fish), accompanied by burghul – the usual grain – or, less frequently, by rice.

SPAIN

In Spain, the tapas bar has always been the focal point of every community from the smallest village in Andalucia to the big cities of Madrid and Barcelona. Where and how tapas originated is often disputed, but what is clear is that they have always been most frequently served with sherry, which is of course an Andalucian specialty. It appears that originally a slice of *jamón serrano* (cured ham) was served on a glass of sherry to keep the flies out; *tapa* is the Spanish word for cover or lid. Over a period of time the range of accompaniments has extended to the range available today throughout Spain, but the tradition of serving it with a glass of sherry has remained to this day.

Tapas are similar to appetizers. However, they seem to remain ungoverned by the laws of their counterparts. They are unlimited by size, ingredient or fixed sequence within a meal, and are therefore very difficult to define. The most useful description is that they are entire in themselves; in a larger form they may be served as meals, and in a smaller form as snacks. They may be liquid or solid (a soup is also a tapa), with or without a sauce, complex or simple: they involve the use of almost every ingredient available from beans, rice and vegetables to fresh fish, and shellfish and a host of meats, both cured and fresh. They present a wealth of choice, color, smell and uninhibited experimentation – a chef's delight if ever there was one.

A good tapas bar is an Aladdin's cave of indulgence. Ranged along the top of the bar you will find an assortment of cheeses, shrimp, crabs, scallops, chicken in garlic, tortilla and patatas bravas. From the ceiling are suspended the smoked *serrano* hams (cured in the Sierra Nevada). By tradition they are often spiked in the base with a shafted metal cup to collect the oils. Stacked against the back wall are dusty bottles of red wine. By the early hours of the morning the floor will be littered with paper napkins, pips and crumbs. The informality and versatility of tapas cuisine makes eating it a sociable and relaxed experience.

ITALY

Italian food is typified by relatively simple, unfussy treatment of good-quality ingredients. Pasta is, of course, what everyone thinks of when Italian cuisine is mentioned. Dried pasta of various kinds is available in most grocery stores, but homemade is best and there is no great mystery involved in making simple, Italian-style pasta dough. All it takes is a touch of muscle power for the kneading and rolling – unless, of course, you have a pasta machine which will make light work of pounding the ingredients to a smooth, pliable dough. It really is worth making your own dough, if only for filled pasta such as tortellini and ravioli, in which you can use a variety of fillings. Remember that you can make a large batch of shapes when the mood takes you, fill them and freeze them for future use.

The majority of the pasta recipes in this book do not necessarily need home-made pasta. As a second best, look out for Italian delicatessens offering good-quality flavored pasta and fresh gnocchi. Oriental noodles and pasta dough are also available fresh from specialist grocery stores. Fresh Chinese egg noodles, won ton wrappers and rice sticks have a finer flavor than the dried types and they also freeze extremely well, so it is worth buying a large batch.

PORTUGAL

Portuguese food is robust and generous, designed to sustain hard-working peasants and generate warmth to counteract the harsh winds from the Atlantic and the bitter cold of the mountains. Based on simple ingredients, Portuguese food is essentially unpretentious, with roots firmly based in home cooking and pure, country dishes. Consequently, there are no complicated techniques. Portuguese kitchens are simple with little equipment or utensils. Ovens have only relatively recently become standard in domestic kitchens, so cooking was formerly done on the hob or over a barbecue in the open air.

The cuisine has developed from the imaginative use of accessible local raw materials, plus a touch of exoticism derived from the importation of ingredients brought home by the explorers in the fifteenth and sixteenth centuries. Spices such as pepper, cloves, nutmeg, and cinnamon came from the discovery of new routes to the East and access to the lucrative spice trade, while the discovery and colonization of the New World resulted in corn, bell peppers, chilis, potatoes, sweet potatoes, beans, tomatoes, avocados, vanilla, pumpkin, zucchini, and turkey being introduced. In the Algarve and Alentejo in the south, Moorish influences can be detected in the popularity of, for example, almonds and the many sweet cakes and pastries. In Madeira dishes based on couscous indicate links with North Africa.

Not surprisingly, Portuguese cooks make greater use of chilis and spices than most other European countries. While ubiquitous parsley is a very popular herb, lesser-known cilantro is also very widely used throughout Portugal.

Portugal runs north-south and is mountainous inland with plains bordering its long coastline. With the consequent variations in terrain, climate and available ingredients, the cooking styles and dishes reflect the regional differences.

Trás-os-Montes, in the extreme northwest of Portugal, is a region of high barren plateaux and deeply cut valleys, including the Douro. In general, the climate is unfriendly, the land poor and a living hard to come by. Dishes are therefore hearty and sustaining with plenty of soups and stews. However, in the sheltered valleys, vegetables, orange, lemon, grapefruit, and olive trees, and grapevines are planted, but the pigs which roam on the hillsides are the staple of the local cooking. To preserve the meat for the harsh, spartan days of winter, large quantities are turned into sausages and hams; Chaves is famed for the quality of its ham, Bragança for its sausages.

The most northerly coastal region of the Minho has a similar robust style of cooking with, as in other coastal regions, an abundant and good supply of fish. As the land is more friendly and the soil more productive than in Trás-os-Montes, there is a patchwork of fields and vineyards. These are owned by peasant smallholders who often grow tall, green *couves* (Portuguese cabbage) beneath trellised vines, to make the famous national soup, *caldo verde*.

The three Beira provinces – Alta, Baixa and Litoral (high, low, and coastal respectively) – spread across the center of Portugal. Beira Alta and Beira Baixa are largely mountainous regions so dishes are of the sturdy peasant variety, while Beira Litoral is a low-lying coastal region, stretching along the Atlantic from Oporto, and the food is lighter with, naturally, fish and shellfish. Some of the best Portuguese cheeses are made in Beira Alta.

Further south is Alentejo, the largest province. On its huge undulating plain, wheat fields abound to produce the main source of wealth for the country. It is therefore hardly surprising that the bread-based soups, *açordas*, originate from here. Cork is the second most important source of livelihood and it is claimed that the pork from the pigs which feed around the cook trees has a special flavor. The plain is also home to flocks of sheep that are kept, not for their meat, but for their wool and milk, which is used for cheese. Rice grows in the lagoons along the coastal side of the province.

Sunny Algarve in the south is the most Moorish part of Portugal. The 100-mile coastline was for centuries so cut off from the rest of Portugal in thought and customs that it was known as "the land beyond." The gently rolling coastal plain is known as "the garden of Portugal" as it produces a superb array of vegetables and fruit – tomatoes, beans, onions, bell peppers, bananas, figs, lemons, oranges, tangerines, grapefruit, grapes, pomegranates, apples, pears, and cherries. Almond trees flourish – the nuts are used in marzipan and innumerable sweetmeats. Sugar cane is also grown and rice is cultivated in a patchwork of paddy fields.

Shellfish is wonderful and often inexpensive, and fish dishes are rich and varied; a favorite way of cooking fish is over barbecues on the sandy beaches, either in a clam shell-shaped cooking vessel, *cataplana*, or charcoal-grilled.

Sardines, plump and very fresh, are delicious served on slabs of local bread, accompanied by parsley and sea salt.

INGREDIENTS AND BASIC RECIPES

Arak A Lebanese spirit distilled from grape juice and flavored with aniseed. Similar to Greek ouzo, it is somewhat lighter in flavor and less syrupy in consistency.

Burghul Wheat grain that has been lightly cooked, dried and ground, either to a fine or medium-coarse grade. It is available unhusked (whole wheat) or, , husked (bleached).

Phyllo A pastry made from flour, water and oil originally developed in ancient Greece. It is rolled extremely fine to an almost paper-thin consistency, and is used for both sweet and savory pastries, including baklava. Difficult to make at home, phyllo is available in commercial packets composed of large sheets.

Pomegranate seeds These make their appearance in some Lebanese stuffings and salads, providing a piquant, slightly sour-sweet taste.

Sausages and ham Sausages are widely used in Portuguese cooking and give a distinctive flavor and character to dishes. Unfortunately not many are exported. In some cases there are Spanish equivalents which can be substituted. For example, Spanish chorizo, which is becoming more widely available now, can be used in place of chouriço, and tocino can be used in place of Portuguese toucinho, smoked bacon. Alternatively, buy a piece of smoked bacon and chop it.

Morcela, a type of black pudding, is used in meat and vegetable dishes. If unavailable, Spanish morcilla can be used instead. Presunto is a quite dark, richly flavored smoked ham. It is both used in cooking and eaten thinly sliced with melon or fresh figs as an appetizer. Westphalian ham is a good substitute.

Tahini A paste made from ground toasted sesame seeds emulsified with olive oil, lemon juice and garlic. This basic staple of Lebanese cuisine can be made at home, but is often bought prepared in bottles (preferable to the canned variety). It is used to make dips and other dishes, but can also be used on its own as a dip.

Vine leaves Fresh vine leaves are always preferable, but in their absence vine leaves can be bought in plastic packets or canned and preserved in brine. They must be soaked and drained before they are used.

Mayonnaise

Mayonnaise keeps well if it is covered and refrigerated. It's very easy to make as long as you are aware of the following:

• Add the oil slowly; if it is warmed slightly, it reduces the risk of the sauce curdling.

• If during the making it becomes too thick, add a little vinegar or hot water.

• The sauce must be thoroughly whisked – the easiest way is to make it in a food processor or to use an electric whisk.

If your mayonnaise does curdle, take a clean bowl, add a dessertspoon of boiling water and gradually whisk in the curdled sauce, or take another yolk, thinned with 1 tsp. cold water and whisked well, then gradually whisk into the curdled sauce.

Makes 1¼ cups mayonnaise
◆ *2 egg yolks*
◆ *2 tsp. vinegar*
◆ *salt and pepper*
◆ *⅛ tsp. mustard*
◆ *1¼ cups olive oil*
◆ *approx 2 tsp. boiling water*

Method

Place the yolks, vinegar and seasoning in a bowl or food processor with the mustard. Gradually pour on the oil, very slowly, whisking or whizzing continually. Add the boiling water, whisking well. Correct the seasoning.

For garlic mayonnaise, add 1 tsp. crushed garlic to the egg yolks for every 1¼ cups.

Béchamel Sauce

Béchamel is a basic milk sauce which is lightly flavored with bay and mace.

Makes about 2½ cups
- *1 thick onion slice*
- *1 bay leaf*
- *1 mace blade*
- *2 parsley sprigs*
- *2½ cups milk*
- *3 tbsp. butter*
- *⅓ cup all-purpose flour*
- *salt and pepper (white or black)*

Method

Place the onion, bay leaf, mace and parsley in a saucepan. Add the milk and heat slowly until just boiling. Remove from the heat, cover and leave for 45 minutes. Strain the milk into a jug or basin. Wash the saucepan, then melt the butter and stir in the flour. Slowly pour in the milk, stirring all the time. Continue stirring until the sauce boils, then reduce the heat, if necessary, so that it just simmers. Cook for 3 minutes, stirring occasionally. Add seasoning to taste. If the sauce is not used straightaway, lay a piece of dampened baking parchment directly on its surface to prevent a skin forming.

Fish Stock

- *2 tbsp. butter*
- *2 lb. white fish bones, washed*
- *8 oz. vegetables, such as onion, celery and leek, peeled and roughly chopped*
- *1 bay leaf*
- *juice of ½ lemon*
- *parsley stalks*
- *6 peppercorns*
- *10 cups water*

Method

Melt the butter in a large pan. Add the fish bones, vegetables and flavorings. Cover and sweat for 5 minutes. Add the water, bring to a boil and skim. Simmer for 20 minutes, the strain. If the strained stock is reduced by half the flavor is better.

Pesto Sauce

This traditional Italian sauce should be used in moderation as it has a very strong flavor. Delicious stirred into fresh pasta, pesto sauce can also be added to other sauces and dishes.

Serves 4–6
- *2 garlic cloves, crushed*
- *8 tbsp. chopped fresh basil*
- *2 tbsp. chopped fresh parsley*
- *scant ½ cup pine nuts*
- *1 cup freshly grated Parmesan cheese*
- *⅔ cup extra-virgin olive oil*
- *salt and pepper*

Method

Place all the ingredients in a food processor or blender, and blend until the pesto reaches the desired texture. Stir pesto sauce into freshly cooked pasta tossed in butter and freshly ground black pepper. Serve immediately with extra freshly grated Parmesan cheese.

Chicken Stock

These quantities may also be applied to a beef or veal stock.

- *2 lb. raw bones*
- *10 cups water*
- *8 oz. vegetables, such as onion, celery and leek, washed, peeled and roughly chopped*
- *2 sprigs of thyme*
- *1 bay leaf*
- *parsley stalks*
- *handful of peppercorns*

Method

Chop the bones, removing any fat. Place in a large pot, add the cold water and bring to a boil. Skim any scum from the top of the water, and simmer gently. Add the vegetables, herbs and peppercorns and simmer for at least 3 hours. Skim, strain and either refrigerate for further use or use straightaway. Stocks will keep for 3–4 days in a refrigerator, and will also freeze well.

PASTA-MAKING
TECHNIQUES

Mixing and Kneading

Unlike pastry, pasta dough needs a firm hand and a positive approach to mixing and kneading. The dough will seem very dry and prone to crumbling at first but as you knead it, the oil and egg combine fully with the flour and the ingredients bind together.

◆ Mix the ingredients in the bowl, using a spoon at first, then your hand.

◆ Begin the kneading process in the bowl, bringing the dough together and "wiping" the bowl clean of any crumbs.

◆ Turn the dough out on to a lightly floured, clean surface and knead it into a ball. Add a little flour to the work surface to prevent the dough sticking, but try to keep this to the minimum during kneading.

◆ Once the dough has come together, knead it firmly and rhythmically, pressing it down and out in one movement, then pulling the edge of the dough back in towards the middle in the next movement. Keep turning the dough as you knead it, so that you work it around in a circle rather than constantly pressing and pulling one side. Keep the dough moving and it will not stick to the surface.

◆ The dough is ready when it is smooth and warm. Wrap it in a polythene bag or plastic wrap and set it aside for 15–30 minutes if possible before rolling it out.

Rolling Out

When rolling the dough, try to keep it in the shape you want to end up with. Press the dough flat, forming it into an oblong or square, then roll it out firmly. Lift and "shake out" the dough a few times initially to ensure it does not stick to the surface. As the dough becomes thinner you have to handle it more carefully to avoid splitting it. However, pasta dough is far more durable than pastry and the smoother it becomes as it is rolled, the tougher it is. Dust the surface under the dough with a little flour occasionally, as

necessary, and dust the top, rubbing the flour over the dough with one hand. Continue rolling until the dough is thin and even – a common mistake is to leave the dough too thick, so that it becomes too solid when cooked. For noodles, or pasta which is to be eaten plain or topped with sauce, try to roll out to the thickness of a piece of brown paper.

Make sure the surface under the dough is sifted with flour, then cover the dough completely with plastic wrap and leave for 10 minutes. This relaxes the dough before cutting and prevents the dough from shrinking as it is cut.

Cutting

You need a large, sharp, knife and a large floured platter or tray on which to place the pasta (a clean roasting pan will do). Flour the dough lightly before cutting. Once cut, keep the pasta dusted with flour to prevent it sticking together. Pasta may be dried before cooking by hanging it on a rack or spreading it out. However, it seems to cook well if it is added to boiling water straight after rolling.

Sheets Trim the dough edges so that they are straight, then cut the pasta into squares or oblongs. This is basic lasagne, so cut the dough to suit the size of dish.

Noodles Dust the dough well with flour, then roll it up. Use a sharp knife to cut the roll into ¼ in. wide slices. Shake out the slices as they are cut and they fall into long noodles. Keep the noodles floured and loosely piled on the tray to prevent them from sticking together. Cover loosely with plastic wrap.

Circles or shapes Use cookie cutters and aspic cutters to stamp out circles and shapes.

Squares Trim the dough edges, then use a clean, long ruler to cut the dough into wide strips. Cut these across into squares.

Small squares Use a ruler to cut the dough into 1 in. wide strips, then cut these across into squares. The small squares may be cooked and treated as bought pasta shapes.

Other shapes If you have the time, you can make other shapes by hand. Cut the dough into strips, then into small oblongs or squares. By twisting, pleating or pinching you can make bows, twists, and so on.

Cooking

Pasta should be cooked in enormous quantities of boiling water. Pour water into the pan to three-quarters of its capacity. Add salt and bring the water to a boil. Adding a little oil to the water helps to prevent it from frothing on the surface and boiling over rapidly – the pasta will not stick together if you have a pan which is large enough, and adding oil does little to prevent the pasta sticking in a pan which is too small! Add the pasta when the water is fully boiling, give it a stir and bring the water back to a boil rapidly. Be ready to reduce the heat otherwise the water will froth over. Cook for about 3 minutes for noodles and other types of unfilled pasta. Filled pasta requires longer to allow the filling to cook through.

When cooked, the pasta should be "al dente" (with bite). It should be firm yet tender, not soft or sticky. Drain the cooked pasta at once, pouring it into a large colander. Shake the colander over the sink, then tip the pasta into a hot bowl and add the dressing or sauce. Serve at once.

Storing

Dust the pasta with plenty of flour and place it in a large airtight container in the refrigerator. Cook within 2 days of making or freeze promptly. The unrolled dough may be wrapped and chilled for 1–2 days.

Uncooked fresh pasta freezes well but it is best to roll and cut the dough first. Separate sheets of pasta by interleaving freezer film between them. Flour noodles and pack them loosely in polythene bags, then spread them out fairly flat for freezing.

Do not thaw frozen pasta before cooking, simply add it to boiling water and cook as for fresh pasta. Noodles and most other shapes take about the same time to cook as unfrozen pasta, once the water has come to the boil again. Frozen filled pasta requires extra cooking time.

Cooked lasagne and cannelloni or similar layered pasta dishes freeze well but cooked shapes and noodles tend to have an inferior texture if frozen after cooking.

Pasta Dough

Makes about 1¼ lb. pasta
- *12 oz. strong all-purpose flour*
- *1 tsp. salt*
- *3 eggs*
- *4 tbsp. olive oil*
- *1 tbsp. water*

Mix the flour and salt together in a large bowl. Make a well in the middle, then add the eggs, olive oil and water. Use a spoon to mix the eggs, oil and water, gradually working in the flour. When the mixture begins to bind into clumps, knead it together with your hands.

Press the dough into a ball and roll it around the bowl to leave the bowl completely clean of the mixture. Then turn the dough out on a lightly floured, clean surface and knead it thoroughly until it is smooth. Follow the notes on kneading (see page 12), keeping the dough moving and adding the minimum extra flour required to prevent it sticking as you work. Wrap the dough in a polythene bag and leave it to rest for 15–30 minutes before rolling it out. Do not chill the dough as this will make it difficult to handle.

Flavored Pasta

The following may be used with the above recipe.
Herb Add 4 tbsp. chopped mixed fresh herbs to the flour and salt. Suitable herbs include parsley, thyme, sage, tarragon, chives, chervil, marjoram and fennel. Rosemary may be used but only in very small quantities as it is a strongly flavored herb. Balance the delicate herbs against the stronger ones by using less of the latter. Use two, three or more herbs but remember that a delicate herb like dill will be totally lost if combined with many other herbs.

Spinach Wash and trim 8 oz. fresh spinach. Place the damp leaves in a saucepan. Cover tightly and cook over high heat for 5 minutes, shaking the pan often. Turn the spinach into a strainer placed over a basin. Press and squeeze all the juice from the spinach, leaving the leaves as dry as possible. Add 6 tbsp. spinach juice to the pasta and omit the oil and water.

Tomato Add 1 tbsp. concentrated tomato paste, beating it into the eggs.

CHAPTER 1

SOUPS, SNACKS
AND APPETIZERS
. . . .

MUCH OF MEDITERRANEAN FOOD IS IDEALLY SUITED

TO A FIRST COURSE OR SNACK MEAL, PARTICULARLY

THE MEZE DISHES OF GREECE AND THE LEBANON

AND THE TAPAS OF SPAIN. YOU'LL FIND A VARIETY

OF DISHES IN THIS CHAPTER TO SUIT ALL OCCASIONS,

FROM HEARTY SOUPS TO SIMPLE SEAFOOD.

Portuguese Gazpacho

This is very similar to Spanish gazpacho, but it contains more bread so is more substantial.

Serves 6

- *1¼ lb. well-flavored tomatoes, peeled, seeded, and finely chopped*
- *1 red bell pepper, cored, seeded, and finely diced*
- *1 green bell pepper, cored, seeded, and finely diced*
- *¼ cucumber, peeled, seeded, and finely diced*
- *3 garlic cloves, crushed*
- *4 tbsp. white wine vinegar*
- *4 tbsp. olive oil*
- *½ tsp. finely chopped oregano*
- *salt and pepper*
- *4 slices day-old firm country bread, crusts removed, cubed*
- *3–4¼ cups iced water*

Method

Put the tomatoes, bell peppers, and cucumber in a soup tureen or large bowl.

Whisk together the garlic, vinegar, oil, oregano, and seasoning; then stir into the tomato mixture with the bread.

Stir in enough iced water to make a thick soup. Chill thoroughly before serving.

Right : Portuguese Gazpacho

Bread Soup with Garlic and Eggs

Açordas are thick, substantial, bread-based Portuguese soups made from readily available, cheap ingredients. They were intended to sustain peasants during, or after, a hard day's toil. Every scrap of bread, including hard, dry crusts, was saved to make a soup. Beggars used to go around with little bags in the hope of such scraps so they could just add easily obtainable water, oil, and garlic to make a warming dish to fill themselves up. An *açorda* could be an appetite-blunting appetizer, or, when times were very hard, it could be the main course. *Açordas* are similar to the "dry soups" of Mexico.

This is the most well-known version of açorda; it is very simple and relies on good chicken stock and good bread.

Serves 4–6

- *1 Spanish onion, quite finely chopped*
- *5 garlic cloves, chopped*
- *1–2 fresh red chilis, seeded and chopped*
- *3–4 tbsp. olive oil*
- *½ lb. day-old good, firm country bread, crumbled*
- *5 cups boiling good chicken stock*
- *4–6 eggs, lightly beaten*
- *handful of chopped cilantro or parsley*
- *salt and pepper*

Method

Cook the onion, garlic, and chilis gently in the oil until the onion has softened. Stir in the bread, raise the heat and cook, stirring, until the bread is lightly browned.

Stir in the stock, lower the heat and stir in the eggs, cilantro or parsley, and seasoning. Serve immediately before the soup boils.

Chicken Soup with Egg and Lemon Sauce

This tangy soup from Greece is deliciously light and refreshing. It is hearty enough for a winter soup, yet zesty enough to be served in the summer, too.

Serves 6

- ◆ 3½ lb. oven-ready chicken, without giblets
- ◆ 1 large onion
- ◆ 2 cloves
- ◆ 2½ qt. water
- ◆ salt and pepper
- ◆ 1⅓ cups long-grain rice
- ◆ 2 eggs
- ◆ juice of 1 lemon

Method

Place the chicken in a large saucepan with the onion, cloves, water and seasoning. Slowly bring the contents of the pan to a boil, skimming off the foam as it appears. Simmer for 2½–3 hours, or until the meat comes away from the bones easily.

Remove from the heat. Lift the chicken out of the pan and place on a chopping board. Remove the onion and cloves from the pan with a slotted spoon and discard. Using a carving knife and fork, take the meat off the bones of the chicken and cut or shred into bite-sized pieces. Discard the bones.

Return the chicken pieces to the saucepan and gently bring the soup back to a boil. Add the rice, cover the pan and simmer the soup for 15–20 minutes, or until the rice is tender.

In a medium-sized bowl, beat together the eggs and lemon juice until frothy. Add 4–5 ladlefuls of the soup to the egg mixture, beating vigorously after each addition. Pour the egg mixture into the saucepan and stir continuously with a wooden spoon until evenly combined. Adjust the seasoning, if necessary. Serve immediately.

Sausage and Tomato Soup

This is a characteristically hearty, warming soup from Portugal. In the absence of the authentic sausages, use good-quality ones from a reputable delicatessen.

Serves 6

- ◆ 2 slices bacon, chopped
- ◆ 8 oz. garlic-flavored smoked sausage
- ◆ 8 oz. morcela sausage or black pudding
- ◆ 1 Spanish onion, halved and sliced
- ◆ 2 garlic cloves, crushed
- ◆ 2¼ lb. well-flavored tomatoes, chopped
- ◆ 1 bay leaf
- ◆ 4¼ cups vegetable or chicken stock or water
- ◆ salt and pepper
- ◆ firm country bread, to serve

Method

Cook the bacon gently in a heavy-based saucepan until the fat has been rendered.

Prick the sausages and cook with the bacon for a few minutes, stirring two or three times, before stirring in the onion and garlic. Cook until softened; then add the tomatoes, bay leaf, and stock or water.

Bring to a boil and simmer gently, uncovered, for about 30 minutes.

Remove the sausages and slice, return to the pan, reheat and season. Serve with firm country bread.

Right : Sausage and Tomato Soup

Lebanese Spring Vegetable Soup

In the Lebanon, when the fresh spring vegetables come into season – particularly the prized fava bean – they find their way into soups like this one.

Serves 6

- *1 cup chicken stock*
- *1 Spanish onion, finely chopped*
- *2 small garlic cloves, crushed*
- *2 stalks celery, finely chopped*
- *salt and pepper*
- *2 leeks, topped, cleaned and thinly sliced into strips*
- *5 artichoke hearts, chopped*
- *1¼ cups shelled fava beans (or lima beans, if unavailable)*
- *4 tbsp. finely chopped mint*
- *4 tbsp. finely chopped cilantro*
- *4 tbsp. finely chopped flat-leaved parsley*
- *cayenne pepper*
- *pita bread, split in half lengthwise, toasted and torn into shreds*

Method

In a large saucepan, combine the chicken stock, onion, garlic cloves, celery and seasoning to taste. Add 1½ cups of water to the pan. Bring the mixture to a boil, then reduce the heat and simmer for about 15 minutes.

Add the leeks, artichoke hearts, and fava beans, and simmer for 35 minutes or until the beans are tender. Take off the heat, and stir in the fresh herbs and cayenne to taste.

Allow the herbs to infuse in the soup for a few minutes, then serve with the shredded, toasted pita scattered over the top.

Chilled Artichoke Soup

This Lebanese soup is refreshing on a hot day. The thistle-like artichoke grows well in the sandier, poorer soils outside the main vegetable-producing Bekkah Valley. In Lebanon, whole small artichokes would be used, but frozen – or even a good brand of canned – artichoke bottoms will do in countries with less profusion!

Serves 6

- *4 cups chicken stock*
- *10–12 frozen or canned artichoke bottoms in brine, drained and coarsely chopped*
- *¾ cup whipping cream*
- *4 tsp. lemon juice*
- *salt and pepper*
- *cayenne pepper*
- *1 small red bell pepper, cored, seeded and finely chopped*
- *8 scallions, white parts only, finely chopped*

Method

In a large saucepan, combine the stock and the chopped frozen or canned artichokes. Bring to a boil, reduce the heat, cover and simmer for about 10 minutes. Remove from the heat and purée in batches in a blender or food processor fitted with a metal blade. Rub the purée through a strainer into a large bowl and allow to cool somewhat. Stir in the cream and lemon juice; add salt, pepper and cayenne to taste. Cover and chill overnight.

Before serving, taste the soup and adjust the seasoning, if necessary. Divide the soup among 6 bowls and serve, garnished with a sprinkling of red bell pepper and scallions.

Green Soup

In this soup from Portugal the green is provided by *couve gallega*, a type of cabbage similar to kale, that has large, deep green leaves. The secret of a good *caldo verde* (green soup) is to shred the leaves extremely finely. As *caldo verde* is so much a part of everyday life in Portugal, market stalls sell large bags of ready-sliced *couve gallega*. You can also buy a hand-turned machine in Portugal like a giant pencil sharpener to do the job for you. This most basic of soups, despite its simplicity, is delicious and another of those comforting dishes to warm the heart. With good bread it makes a substantial main course in its own right, but in Portugal it is often served as an appetizer. It keeps well and is just as nice, if not better, reheated.

Serves 4

◆ *2¼ lb. potatoes, cut into smallish pieces if large*
◆ *2 garlic cloves, coarsely chopped*
◆ *7 cups light chicken stock or water*
◆ *1 lb. spring cabbage or Savoy cabbage*
◆ *8 oz. chouriço sausage, sliced (optional)*
◆ *salt and pepper*
◆ *4–6 tbsp. olive oil, to serve*
◆ *1 tbsp. cilantro leaves, to serve (optional)*

Method

Put the potatoes, garlic, and stock or water into a large saucepan, bring to a boil and simmer for 15 minutes, or until tender.

Meanwhile, remove the stems from the cabbage leaves. Roll the leaves into tubes and then cut across them to shred as thinly as possible.

Mash the potatoes and garlic together in the saucepan to form a fairly smooth purée. Add the cabbage and sausage, if using, and simmer for about 5 minutes, until warmed through. Season to taste.

Ladle into warmed soup bowls and swirl some olive oil into each portion. Scatter over cilantro leaves, if using, and serve.

Spinach and Yogurt Soup

Popular in Egypt, Jordan and Lebanon, this soup is usually made with beet greens, which impart a characteristic, slightly sour, flavor. When the more easily obtainable spinach is used, as in this recipe, a touch of light white wine vinegar will help to approximate the taste.

Serves 6

- ◆ *1 garlic clove, crushed*
- ◆ *2 cups Greek-style yogurt*
- ◆ *large pinch turmeric*
- ◆ *3 tbsp. olive oil*
- ◆ *1 large onion, finely chopped*
- ◆ *1 lb. spinach leaves, washed thoroughly and shredded*
- ◆ *2 small leeks, finely chopped*
- ◆ *¼ cup long-grain rice*
- ◆ *1 cup vegetable stock*
- ◆ *3 tbsp. white wine vinegar (champagne vinegar, if available)*
- ◆ *salt and pepper*

Method

In a bowl, whisk together the garlic, yogurt and turmeric. Set aside to let the flavors mingle.

Heat the olive oil in a large casserole and stir in the onion. Sauté until lightly colored and softened, then stir in the spinach, leeks and rice. When the spinach has wilted and the rice is coated, pour in the vegetable stock and the vinegar. Season to taste. Bring to a boil, then reduce the heat, cover and simmer for about 15–20 minutes, until the rice is tender.

Just before serving, take the soup off the heat. Whisk in the yogurt mixture, and then ladle immediately into bowls.

Tomato and Cilantro Soup

Cilantro is a familiar herb in Lebanese dishes, to which it imparts a tang far more appealing than its rather foetid smell would suggest. This is a summer soup, using the lush tomatoes of the inland valleys, and would make an excellent preliminary to a fish or poultry main dish.

Serves 6

- ◆ *3 lb. ripe, plump tomatoes, roughly chopped*
- ◆ *1 small onion*
- ◆ *¼ cup tomato juice*
- ◆ *3 tbsp. freshly squeezed orange juice*
- ◆ *1 Greek or Italian pickled pepper, seeded*
- ◆ *¼ tsp. superfine sugar*
- ◆ *ice water*
- ◆ *4 tbsp. finely chopped cilantro*
- ◆ *⅛ cup Greek-style yogurt*

Method

In a blender or food processor fitted with a metal blade, purée the chopped tomatoes, onion, tomato juice, orange juice, pepper and sugar until the mixture is as smooth as possible.

Press the purée through a strainer, rubbing with a wooden spoon to force as much through as possible. Discard the residue, and add enough ice water to thin the purée to a soup-like consistency. Stir in the cilantro, cover and chill until cold. Pass the yogurt separately at the table, to allow guests to add as much of it as they wish.

Left : Spinach and Yogurt Soup

Classic Greek Vegetable Soup

Serve this classic Greek soup with olive bread.

Serves 6–8

- ♦ ½ cup olive oil
- ♦ 2 garlic cloves, crushed
- ♦ 2 onions, finely chopped
- ♦ 2½ cups finely shredded cabbage
- ♦ 3 carrots, chopped
- ♦ 3 celery stalks, chopped
- ♦ 2 large potatoes, peeled and diced
- ♦ 2½ qt. vegetable stock or water
- ♦ 4 tomatoes, peeled, seeded and chopped
- ♦ salt and pepper
- ♦ 4 tbsp. chopped fresh parsley
- ♦ 2 oz. feta or kefalotyri cheese, grated

Method

Heat the olive oil in a large saucepan and add the garlic and onion. Cook for 5 minutes, until the onion is softened but not colored. Add the cabbage and continue to cook for another 3–4 minutes.

Add the carrots and celery to the saucepan, stir and cook for a further 5 minutes. Add the potatoes, stir and cook gently for another 5 minutes, until the vegetables are softened.

Pour in the vegetable stock or water and stir well. Increase the heat to bring the soup to a boil. Cover and simmer for 12–15 minutes. Add the tomatoes and season to taste with salt and pepper. Re-cover and gently simmer the soup for about 1 hour. Stir in the parsley just before the end of the cooking time. Serve sprinkled with grated cheese.

Sidon Melon Soup

Melons of all types – green, yellow and orange – grow profusely on the small farms of the inland valleys of the Lebanon. When at their peak, they are pleasing simply cut in half or quarters. This ingenious two-tone soup can make use of slightly over-ripe fruit.

Serves 6

- *2 large ogen melons, peeled, seeded and chopped*
- *4 tbsp. lime juice*
- *4 tbsp. superfine sugar*
- *2 large cantaloupe melons, peeled, seeded and chopped*
- *4 tbsp. lemon juice*
- *½ cup Greek-style yogurt*
- *ground cinnamon*
- *mint leaves*

Method

In a blender or food processor fitted with a metal blade, purée the ogen melon, lime juice and 2 tbsp. sugar until smooth. Pour into a pitcher, cover and chill until cold.

Rinse out the bowl of the processor or blender and fill with the cantaloupe melon, lemon juice and remaining sugar. Purée until smooth. Pour into a pitcher, cover and chill until cold.

When ready to serve, position each soup bowl in front of you. Pick up both pitchers, and pour the two soups into the bowl at the same time, one on each side. Repeat with the remaining bowls.

Each soup will be two-tone; use a spoon to feather the edges gently to obtain a softer effect. Top each serving with a dollop of yogurt sprinkled lightly with cinnamon and garnished with a sprig of mint.

Fried Cheese

Served with a glass of ouzo, this dish is a classic simple meze from Greece.

Serves 4–6
- *8 oz. Haloumi cheese*
- *½ cup all-purpose flour*
- *pepper*
- *¼ cup olive oil*
- *2 tbsp. lemon juice*

Method

Cut the cheese into slices 3 inches long and ½ inch thick. Rinse the slices of cheese under cold running water and pat dry on paper towels.

Place the flour on a plate and season with the pepper. Toss the slices of cheese in the flour to coat evenly.

Heat the olive oil in a heavy-based skillet and cook the slices of cheese in batches, shaking off the excess flour before frying. Cook for 2–3 minutes on each side, then transfer to a warm plate and pat with paper towels to soak up any excess oil, if necessary.

Sprinkle the cheese with the lemon juice and serve immediately.

Cheese Balls

In Lebanon, these cheese balls would be made of a salted Feta-like goat cheese called *gibna arish*. Here, an unripened chèvre log leavened with Feta makes a very acceptable alternative.

Makes 25–30 balls
- *8 oz. log unripened chèvre cheese*
- *6 oz. Feta cheese*
- *½ tsp. ground cumin*
- *¼ tsp. cayenne pepper*
- *3 tbsp. finely chopped mint or thyme leaves*
- *4 tbsp. olive oil*

Method

Combine the cheeses, cumin and cayenne in a bowl and mash together thoroughly. Take out small spoonfuls of cheese and form into bite-sized balls. Roll the balls in the chopped herbs and chill until firm. Before serving, mound the balls on a plate and drizzle the olive oil over them.

Cheese Phyllo Triangles

A classic Greek meze dish. Why not double the quantity and freeze half before baking – then you'll have something to fall back on when unexpected guests drop in.

Serves 8–10
- ◆ 8 oz. Feta cheese
- ◆ ¾ cup cottage cheese
- ◆ 2 eggs, beaten
- ◆ 2 tbsp. chopped fresh parsley
- ◆ 1 tbsp. chopped fresh mint
- ◆ salt and pepper
- ◆ 8 oz. phyllo pastry dough, thawed if frozen
- ◆ 1 cup butter, melted

Method

Preheat the oven to 400°F. Place the Feta and cottage cheese in a bowl and mix. Beat in the eggs, parsley and mint. Season to taste.

To make the triangles, lay the phyllo pastry dough out on the work surface and cover with a slightly damp cloth. Separate the first sheet of dough and lay it on the work surface, keeping the remaining sheets covered to prevent them drying out. Divide into three equal strips and brush each strip lightly with the melted butter.

Place 2 teaspoons of the cheese mixture toward the bottom right-hand corner of the dough strip. Fold that corner diagonally over to the top left-hand corner, to make a triangle. Then take the bottom left-hand corner and fold it diagonally over to the top right-hand corner, and so on, alternately folding the bottom corners in a diagonal pattern to finish up with a neat triangle. Place on a buttered cookie sheet.

Repeat the process with the other strips and then continue with another sheet of dough.

Bake in the oven for 15–20 minutes, or until lightly golden and crisp. Transfer to a wire rack and serve warm, or allow to cool.

Stuffed Vine Leaves

Stuffed vine leaves are popular all over the eastern Mediterranean crescent, from Greece to Egypt. Unlike some of these nationalities, however, the Lebanese prefer their stuffing without meat and served cold.

Makes 30–50 stuffed vine leaves

- 6 oz. packet vine leaves (about 35)
- 4 tbsp. olive oil
- 2 tbsp. pine nuts
- 1 large onion, finely chopped
- ⅓ cup long-grain rice
- salt and pepper
- 1 tbsp. raisins
- 1½ tbsp. finely chopped mint
- ½ tbsp. cinnamon
- juice of 2 lemons
- lemon wedges, to serve

Method

Remove the vine leaves from the packet, separate them, place in a large container and pour boiling water over them. Allow to soak

for 15 minutes, then drain. Return to the bowl, pour cold water on them, soak for a further 10 minutes, then drain thoroughly on paper towels.

Heat 1 tablespoon of the olive oil in a large skillet. Add the pine nuts and sauté, stirring, for about 4 minutes, or until the nuts are golden. Remove the pine nuts with a slotted spoon and reserve. Add another tablespoon of oil to the pan, and stir in the onion. Sauté until limp and lightly colored, about 5–6 minutes, then add the rice and salt and pepper to taste. Stir the rice until it is coated with the oil, then pour in ½ cup boiling water to cover. Reduce the heat, cover, and cook over medium heat for about 5 minutes. Take off the heat and allow to sit until the water has been absorbed, and the rice is tender – about 20 minutes. Stir in the raisins, pine nuts, chopped mint and cinnamon.

Lay a vine leaf flat, and spoon 2 tablespoons of the rice mixture near the stem end. Roll the leaf one turn over the mixture, then tuck in the sides of the leaf toward the center. Continue to roll the leaf like a cigar, until you reach the end. Squeeze the bundle to remove excess moisture. Repeat the process with the remaining leaves and stuffing.

If there are any vine leaves left over, lay them on the bottom of a lightly oiled casserole. Arrange the stuffed leaves in a single layer on top. Pour over the lemon juice and just enough hot water to cover. Drizzle over the remaining 2 tablespoons of olive oil. Weight the stuffed leaves down with a plate. Cover tightly and cook over high heat for about 4 minutes, then lower the heat and simmer for about 40 minutes. Remove from the heat, uncover and allow to cool in the cooking liquid. When cold, remove the stuffed leaves with a slotted spoon and arrange on a platter.

Stuffed Green Bell Peppers with Chili Mince

A Spanish variation on stuffed bell peppers with chilis to add some fierceness.

Serves 4
- *1 onion, finely chopped*
- *¼ cup oil or butter*
- *1 lb. ground beef or pork*
- *2 tsp. crushed garlic*
- *6 red chilis, finely chopped*
- *½ tsp. chopped fresh oregano*
- *1 bay leaf*
- *2½ cups water*
- *salt and pepper*
- *2 tsp. tomato paste*
- *1 tsp. chopped fresh basil*
- *2 large tomatoes, peeled and chopped*
- *8 oz. can kidney beans*
- *3 large or 6 small green bell peppers*
- *½ cup grated Manchego cheese*

Method
Gently cook the onion in the oil or butter.

Add the meat, garlic, chilis, oregano, bay leaf, water, salt, pepper, tomato paste and basil, and cook, stirring, until it reaches a boil.

Lower the heat and simmer for 45 minutes, stirring occasionally.

Add the tomatoes and beans, season to taste and bring to a boil. Remove from the heat.

Preheat the oven to 400°F. To prepare the bell peppers, remove the stalks. Plunge into boiling salted water and simmer for 5 minutes. Immediately cool in cold water and drain.

If the bell peppers are large, cut in half lengthwise, and remove the seeds. Fill with meat mixture. Sprinkle with cheese, place on a baking tray in the oven and bake until the cheese melts.

If the bell peppers are small, cut off the tops and set them aside. Carefully remove the seeds and cores. Trim the bases so that the bell peppers will sit squarely, without making holes in them.

Fill with meat mixture and sprinkle with cheese.

Place on a baking tray with the tops next to them to heat up. When the cheese is melted, replace the tops and serve.

Tuna Fish with Garbanzo Beans

This wonderful, summery combination of tuna fish and garbanzo beans from Greece makes an excellent cold meze dish. It's also a quick, easy and nutritious idea for a light lunch.

Serves 4–6
- ◆ 15-oz. can garbanzo beans
- ◆ 15-oz. can tuna fish in brine
- ◆ 4 scallions, finely chopped
- ◆ 1 celery stalk, finely chopped
- ◆ ½ cup olive oil
- ◆ 4 tbsp. lemon juice
- ◆ finely grated zest of ½ lemon
- ◆ 3 tbsp. chopped fresh parsley
- ◆ 1 tbsp. chopped fresh dill
- ◆ salt and pepper
- ◆ 2 garlic cloves, crushed
- ◆ ¼ tsp. dry mustard
- ◆ fresh parsley and dill, to garnish

Method
Drain the garbanzo beans and tuna fish and place in a medium-sized bowl. Gently stir in the scallions and celery.

Combine the oil, lemon juice and zest, parsley, dill, salt and pepper, garlic and dry mustard together in a screwtop jar. Shake well to mix, then pour over the garbanzo beans and tuna fish. Stir gently to combine, then turn the mixture out on to a serving plate. For the best results, cover and chill for several hours before serving. Garnish with fresh herbs.

Mussels and Beans with Tomato

This hearty dish from Spain makes a filling appetizer or a light lunch.

Serves 4–6
- 2 lb. white navy beans
- 2 tbsp. olive oil
- 1 onion, chopped
- 2 slices good bacon, chopped
- 2 tsp. crushed garlic
- 5 cups chicken stock (see p.11)
- 2 lb. mussels, washed and debearded
- 1 large tomato, peeled and chopped
- 1 tbsp. parsley, chopped
- juice of 1 lemon
- salt and pepper

Method

Soak the beans overnight in cold water, or buy canned beans.

Heat the oil and sweat the onion in it until soft. Add the bacon and stir.

Add the beans and garlic, cover with the chicken stock and cook (20 minutes for canned beans, 2 hours for dried, soaked beans).

Add the mussels, shake, cover and cook until the mussels open. Discard any that don't.

Stir in the tomato, parsley and lemon juice. Season and serve in small bowls.

Ceviche of Shrimp

A Spanish tapas recipe in which the marinade gives a bite to the shrimp.

Serves 4

- ◆ *2 lb. shrimp or 1 lb. shrimp and 1 lb. white fish, skinned and cleaned*
- ◆ *5 cups water*
- ◆ *2½ cups lime juice*
- ◆ *2 red onions, chopped*
- ◆ *2 tbsp. soy sauce*
- ◆ *salt and pepper*
- ◆ *2 cucumbers, seeded, skinned, halved lengthwise and cut into half moons*
- ◆ *1 red bell pepper, seeded and thinly sliced*
- ◆ *1 bunch of dill, chopped*
- ◆ *Tabasco sauce, to taste*
- ◆ *lime wedges, to garnish*

Method

Place the shrimp in a large bowl.

Mix the ingredients for the marinade together (water, lime juice, red onions, soy sauce, salt and pepper) and pour over the shrimp. Marinate for 20 minutes.

Add the cucumber, bell pepper slices and dill and toss. Spoon onto plates or into small bowls.

Sprinkle with pepper and Tabasco sauce. Serve with lime wedges.

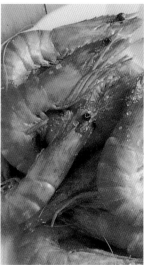

Shrimp with Garlic, Oil, and Chili Sauce

In this Portuguese recipe the garlic and chilis not only flavor the shrimp, but also the oil. The shrimp gives the oil yet more flavor, making a delicious sauce that begs to be mopped up by good bread. Use your fingers to peel the shrimp.

Serves 3–4
- ◆ 6 tbsp. olive oil
- ◆ 4 garlic cloves, finely crushed
- ◆ 2 dried red chilis, seeded and crumbled
- ◆ 1 lb. uncooked large shrimp in their shells
- ◆ sea salt

Method
Heat the oil in a pan, add the garlic and chilis, and cook for 1–2 minutes. Then add the shrimp and sea salt to taste. Fry briskly, turning the shrimp over constantly, for 2 minutes.

Serve the shrimp in warmed individual bowls, accompanied by good bread to dip into the flavored oil.

Roasted Bell Pepper Salad

Make this Greek salad look especially pretty by using a mixture of colored bell peppers.

Serves 4

- ◆ *6 bell peppers of various colors*
- ◆ *2 onions, finely chopped*
- ◆ *salt and pepper*
- ◆ *3 tbsp. white wine vinegar*
- ◆ *¼ cup olive oil*
- ◆ *3 tbsp. chopped fresh parsley, to garnish*

Method

Preheat the oven to 450°F. Place the whole bell peppers on a cookie sheet and roast in the oven for 20–25 minutes, or until the bell peppers have wilted and turned soft.

Allow the bell peppers to cool slightly, then peel away the skins and slice the bell peppers in half. Scrape out the seeds and cut off the stems.

Slice the bell pepper flesh into strips and place on a serving plate. Sprinkle the onion, salt and pepper, vinegar and olive oil over the top. Garnish with chopped parsley and chill before serving.

Salt Cod with Green Bell Peppers and Potatoes

Salt cod is a perennial favorite in Spain. It needs a bit of preparation but is well worth the trouble.

Serves 4
- 1½ lb. dried salt cod, chopped into bite-sized pieces
- 2 tbsp. olive oil
- 1 large onion, chopped
- 1 celery stalk, chopped
- 1 medium green bell pepper, seeded and finely sliced
- 1 large leek, washed and chopped
- 1 tsp. crushed garlic
- 4 medium potatoes, washed and sliced into ½ in. thick rounds
- 1 glass of dry white wine
- 1½ cups fish stock (see p.11)
- pepper
- 1 tbsp. chopped parsley

Method
Soak the salt cod for 24 hours, with at least 3 changes of water. Cut into 2-inch pieces.

Heat the oil in a pot, and gently cook the onion, celery and green bell pepper.

Add the leek, garlic, potatoes and wine. Reduce the wine by one-half.

Add the stock, cover with a lid and simmer until the vegetables are soft. You may need a bit more liquid; if so, add a little water.

Add the cod and plenty of pepper. Stir and cook for a further 6–8 minutes.

Serve the fish in shallow bowls, with plenty of sauce and chopped parsley.

Fried Sardines

The taste of fresh sardines is truly a taste of the Mediterranean. This Spanish recipe adds some zing.

Method

Take the sardines (if the head is on, leave it) and cut through the bellies lengthwise without cutting through the bone. Butterfly the fish.

Blend the marinade ingredients together and brush on the fish. Leave for 20 minutes.

Shake the flour over the fish, dusting until well covered. Shake off any excess flour.

Heat the oil until hot and fry the sardines, turning to brown both sides.

To prepare the sauce/dip, mix all the ingredients together, then either spoon onto the plates with the sardines, or use as a dip.

Serves 3–4
- ◆ *12 sardines (about 4 in. long)*
- ◆ *½ cup seasoned flour*

Marinade
- ◆ *2 tsp. chopped parsley*
- ◆ *4 tbsp. lemon juice*
- ◆ *½ tsp. crushed garlic*
- ◆ *salt and pepper*
- ◆ *4 tbsp. olive oil*

Sauce/Dip
- ◆ *salt and pepper*
- ◆ *1 large tomato, skinned and chopped*
- ◆ *1 small green bell pepper, seeded and chopped*
- ◆ *1 oz. onion, chopped*
- ◆ *enough mayonnaise (see p.10), to bind*

Patatas Bravas

Roast potatoes with a slightly sweet hot sauce poured over them are a favorite tapas dish in Spain.

Serves 4–6
- *1 onion, chopped*
- *2 tbsp. olive oil*
- *1 bay leaf*
- *2 red chilis*
- *2 tsp. crushed garlic*
- *1 tbsp. tomato paste*
- *½ tbsp. sugar (up to 1 tbsp. if the sauce is too tart for your liking)*
- *1 tbsp. soy sauce*
- *1 lb. can plum tomatoes, chopped*
- *1 glass of white wine*
- *salt and pepper*
- *8 medium potatoes*

Method
To make the sauce, sweat the onion in the oil with the bay leaf.

When soft, add the chilis, garlic, tomato paste, sugar and soy sauce. Sweat for a further 5 minutes on a low heat.

Add the chopped tomatoes and white wine. Stir and bring to a boil. Simmer for 10 minutes. Taste and season. This sauce should be slightly sweet; the flavor of the tomatoes should not dominate it.

Preheat the oven to 450°F. Cut the potatoes like small roast potatoes. Grease a baking tray. Season the potatoes well and brush with melted butter. Roast in the oven until golden.Pour the tomato sauce over the potatoes and serve.

Cold Eggplant Purée

This Lebanese dip combines two smoky flavors: that of the broiled eggplant and that of the tahini or sesame paste.

Makes about 2 cups
- *2 medium eggplants, cut in half*
- *juice of 1 lemon*
- *2 garlic cloves, crushed*
- *3 tbsp. tahini*
- *½ tsp. ground cumin*
- *salt and pepper*
- *1 tsp. chopped flat-leaved parsley*
- *black olives*

Method
Prick the skins of the halved eggplants and place them flesh down on a greased baking sheet. Place them under a hot broiler for about 15–20 minutes, until the skins are blackened and the flesh is soft.

Remove them from the broiler, plunge them into cold water, then skin thoroughly, cutting off the skin if it sticks.

Roughly chop the eggplant flesh, and put it into a food processor fitted with a metal blade. Add the lemon juice and process for a few seconds, until combined. Scrape the mixture down the sides of the bowl and add the garlic, tahini, cumin, and salt and pepper to taste. Process the mixture until it becomes a smooth purée.

Turn the purée into a bowl, cover and chill slightly. Before serving, swirl the top attractively and sprinkle with the chopped parsley and a few black olives. Serve with Arab bread (*khoubz*) or pita.

Garlic Mushrooms

A simple Spanish snack or appetizer that's always a popular choice.

Serves 4
- ◆ 6 tbsp. butter
- ◆ 1½ lb. mushrooms, button or cap
- ◆ a few drops of lemon juice
- ◆ salt and pepper
- ◆ 3 tsp. crushed garlic
- ◆ 1 tbsp. chopped cilantro or parsley

Method

Heat the butter in a large pan.

Add the mushrooms and sweat gently, covered, for 5 minutes, shaking occasionally.

Add the lemon juice, salt and pepper.

Increase the heat, tossing the mushrooms well.

Add the garlic, toss and cook for 2 minutes.

Add the cilantro or parsley and cook for 1 minute. Remove from the heat and serve.

Marinated Meatballs

These mouthwatering, bite-sized Greek morsels are an essential addition to any meze table. However many you make, they are sure to all be eaten up.

Serves 4
- ◆ 10 oz. lean ground beef
- ◆ 1 cup fresh white bread crumbs
- ◆ 1 egg, beaten
- ◆ 1 tsp. mustard
- ◆ 1 tbsp. chopped fresh parsley
- ◆ pinch of dried oregano
- ◆ 1 onion, grated
- ◆ salt and pepper
- ◆ 1 tsp. dried mint
- ◆ pinch each of ground cinnamon and cloves
- ◆ 2 garlic cloves, crushed
- ◆ olive oil, for greasing
- ◆ 15-oz. can chopped tomatoes
- ◆ ¼ cup water
- ◆ chopped fresh parsley and mint, to garnish

Method

Preheat the oven to 450°F. Combine all the ingredients, except the canned tomatoes and water, in a large mixing bowl. Mix thoroughly. With slightly damp hands, shape the mixture into 1-inch balls and place on a lightly oiled cookie sheet.

Bake for 20 minutes, turning each ball over halfway through the cooking time. Drain the meatballs on paper towels, then transfer to a large, shallow baking dish. Set aside.

Place the canned tomatoes in a food processor or blender and purée until smooth. Pass through a strainer to remove the seeds. Pour the strained tomato juice into a small saucepan and add the water. Simmer the sauce for 5 minutes, then pour over the meatballs. Allow to cool, then cover and refrigerate for several hours or overnight.

To heat the meatballs through, place in an oven preheated to 400°F for about 25–30 minutes, stirring once during cooking. Serve garnished with the herbs.

CHAPTER 2

FISH

. . . .

NOT SURPRISINGLY, THIS CUISINE IS RICH IN

FISH DISHES. THE MEDITERRANEAN WAY WITH

PISCATORIAL FOOD OFTEN CONSISTS OF NOTHING

MORE COMPLICATED THAN SUPERBLY FRESH FISH,

A SPLASH OF WINE, A DASH OF GARLIC AND A

SCATTERING OF THE AROMATIC HERBS THAT THRIVE

IN THE POOR SOIL AND SCORCHING SUNSHINE THAT

ARE TYPICAL OF THE REGION.

Portuguese Fish Stew

Most coastal regions of Portugal have their own varieties of a fish stew (stew is really a misnomer as the fish only needs to be cooked gently for a short time), often containing a mixture of both white fish and shellfish.

Serves 4

- 6 tbsp. olive oil
- 1 fairly large onion, chopped
- 5 garlic cloves, crushed
- 3 celery stalks, chopped
- 2 leeks, chopped
- 1 small bulb Florence fennel, chopped
- 1¼ cups chopped well-flavored tomatoes
- 2 tsp. tomato paste
- ½ red bell pepper, cored, seeded, and chopped
- 1 bay leaf
- 2 inch strip orange peel
- 7½ cups fish stock (see p.11)
- 2¼–3 lb. mixed shellfish and fish (except oily varieties), filleted
- large pinch of cayenne pepper
- salt and pepper

Method

Heat the oil in a large saucepan. Add the onion, garlic, celery, leeks, and fennel, and cook slowly until the vegetables are very soft, about 45 minutes.

Add the tomatoes, tomato paste, red bell pepper, bay leaf, and orange peel. Cook briskly, stirring constantly, to dry out the moisture from the tomatoes.

Add the fish stock, bring to a boil and then lower the heat so the liquid simmers. Add the fish and simmer gently for 40 minutes.

Purée the mixture in batches in a blender or food processor. Pass through a strainer, if liked, pushing down well on the strainer to press through as much as possible.

Return the mixture to the pan and add the cayenne pepper and seasoning.
Reheat gently.

Clams with Herbs and Wine

This light, quick Portuguese dish made with clams comes from the Costa de Prata. Serve with good crusty bread to mop up the delicious juices.

Serves 4

- 4 lb. small clams
- 2 tbsp. olive oil
- 1–2 garlic cloves, crushed
- handful of mixed parsley and cilantro with a little oregano
- 1 cup well-flavored tomatoes, skinned, seeded, and chopped
- 4 tbsp. medium-bodied dry white wine
- salt and pepper

Method

Clean, wash, and rinse the clams thoroughly.

Heat the oil in a large saucepan, add the garlic and herbs and cook, stirring frequently, for 2 minutes. Add the clams, tomatoes, and wine. Season, using plenty of pepper.

Bring to a boil, then cover and cook for 3–4 minutes until the clams open.

Right : Clams with Herbs and Wine

Clams or Mussels Tyre Style

Tyre, in the Lebanon, was renowned in ancient times for its purple dye, reserved for Roman aristocrats and derived from the crushed shells of whelks. But that was not the only shellfish that thrived on the sea-shelf fronting the harbor. Mussels, several types of clam, shrimp and crayfish graced the Tyrean table and were transported inland. The tradition remains.

Serves 4–6
- ◆ 1 garlic clove, crushed
- ◆ 1 small red onion, thinly sliced
- ◆ 1 cup white wine
- ◆ 2 lb. clams or small mussels
- ◆ 4 plum tomatoes, peeled, seeded and chopped
- ◆ 2 tbsp. lemon juice
- ◆ 1 tbsp. butter
- ◆ 1 tbsp. finely chopped cilantro

Method

Put the garlic and chopped onion with the wine in a deep saucepan. Bring to a boil, simmer for 2 minutes, then add the clams or mussels. Bring back to a boil, lower the heat and simmer, covered, for about 5 minutes, or until the shellfish open. Discard any clams or mussels that have not opened.

Remove the shellfish to a serving bowl and keep them warm. Add the tomatoes to the cooking liquid, and mash them into it. Bring it back to a boil and reduce slightly. Just before serving, stir in the lemon juice, butter, and cilantro. Pour over the clams or mussels and serve immediately, with khoubz (Arab bread) or pita bread to mop up the sauce.

Clams with Garlic Sausage, Ham, and Cilantro

This spicy, fragrant clam dish comes from the Algarve, in Portugal, where it is cooked in a *cataplana*, a clam-shaped pan traditionally made of copper but now also of aluminum. The lid, which is hinged at the back like a clam shell, is clamped firmly in place by clasps on either side, so the pan can be turned over during cooking with no danger of the contents leaking out. However, the recipe can be cooked successfully in a saucepan or flameproof casserole with a very tight-fitting lid.

Serves 4

- 2 tbsp. olive oil
- 2 onions, chopped
- 1–2 garlic cloves, finely chopped
- 3 oz. chouriço, or other garlic-flavored smoked sausage
- 3 oz. smoked ham, chopped
- about 1 tsp. Piri-piri sauce (see p.64), or hot pepper sauce, to taste
- 2¼ lb. clams
- 1½ tbsp. chopped cilantro
- salt

Method

Heat the oil in a saucepan or flameproof casserole. Add the onions and garlic and cook, stirring occasionally, until softened but not colored.

Stir the sausage, ham, and Piri-piri sauce or hot pepper sauce into the onions. Cover and cook fairly gently, shaking the pan occasionally, for 15 minutes.

Meanwhile, scrub the clams clean and rinse them thoroughly under cold running water.

Add the clams, cilantro and salt to taste to the mixture in the pan. Cover and cook for a further 5–6 minutes, shaking the pan occasionally, until the clams open. Serve from the pan.

Baked Stuffed Fish

This is a Lebanese recipe with many variations. The optional pomegranate seeds are an introduction from Iran, but one that is much appreciated in Lebanon. If the stuffed fish is white-fleshed, it is often served cold with a *Taratoor bi Sonoba* (Pine Nut Sauce, *see opposite*); if an oily fish, it is always served hot, without sauce, simply garnished with lemon wedges.

Serves 6
- *4 lb. sea bass or mullet, cleaned, gutted and scaled (or 6 × 10 oz. whole mackerel)*
- *olive oil*
- *salt and pepper*
- *1 small onion, finely chopped*
- *½ green bell pepper, finely chopped*
- *⅔ cup pine nuts*
- *½ tsp. bruised coriander seeds*
- *½ cup fresh bread crumbs*
- *2–3 tbsp. white raisins*
- *2 tbsp. pomegranate seeds (optional)*
- *5 tbsp. finely chopped flat-leaved parsley*
- *4 tbsp. fresh lemon juice*
- *lemon wedges or Pine Nut Sauce*

Garnish
- *cucumber*
- *olives*
- *tomatoes*
- *green bell peppers*
- *pimento*
- *anchovies*
- *hard-cooked eggs*
- *toasted pine nuts*

Method
If you are stuffing one whole white fish, rub it liberally with olive oil and rub in salt and pepper to taste. Leave to chill for 1 hour.

If using mackerel, do not buy the fish gutted; take them home whole. Sever the heads, leaving them attached by a piece of skin. Snap the tail sharply, breaking the backbone and roll it back and forth to loosen.

Using a spoon, scoop out the innards of the fish, and follow this by drawing out the loosened backbone. Use the spoon to press the flesh against the sides of the fish, enlarging the hole for stuffing. Wash the fish inside and out, pat dry and set aside.

To make the stuffing, heat 3 tablespoons olive oil. Sauté the onion for about 5 minutes over medium heat, stirring, until softened. Add the green bell pepper and continue stirring, until it is soft and the onions are changing color. Stir in the pine nuts for another 2 minutes, then the crushed coriander seeds and bread crumbs. Stir for about 1 minute. Remove the pan from the heat and add the raisins, pomegranate seeds (if used) and the parsley. Season the stuffing with salt and pepper to taste, and moisten it with 1 tablespoon lemon juice.

Preheat the oven to 400°F. Stuff the large white fish or the smaller mackerel with the mixture. Secure the white fish with a little thread or small skewers; fill the mackerel through the top opening and replace the heads as well as possible. Arrange the fish on a baking sheet and pour over the remaining lemon juice (and more oil on the white fish, if this is necessary).

Place the fish in the oven and bake, covered loosely with foil, for about 40–45 minutes for the whole fish, or about 30 minutes for the mackerel.

Remove from the oven. Serve the mackerel immediately with lemon wedges; the white fish may also be served hot or cold served with the Pine Nut Sauce.

In the latter case, the fish is usually garnished with paper-thin cucumber slices, olive rings, tomato roses with green bell pepper leaves, pimento and anchovy strips, hard-cooked egg slices and toasted pine nuts.

Pine Nut Sauce

This is a sauce that is usually partnered with fish, although to Western tastes it marries well with pasta, veal and poultry dishes. Although it is most usually served cold, it can also be used in cooking fish or meat.

Makes about 1½ cups
- 1 garlic clove, crushed
- salt
- 2 slices white bread, crusts removed and cubed
- 2 cups pine nuts
- ¼ tsp. cayenne pepper
- juice of 2 lemons

Method
Mash the garlic as much as possible in a bowl with a pinch of salt. Add the bread cubes, cover with warm water to soak and leave for 10 minutes.

Meanwhile place the pine nuts in the grinder of a blender, or in the bowl of a food processor fitted with a metal blade. When the nuts are finely chopped (if using the grinder, transfer the nuts to a liquidizing bowl), add the soaked bread, squeezed to remove some of the moisture, and the cayenne. Process a short time, then add the lemon juice, a little at a time, with the processor on. The result should be a rich, creamy sauce. If necessary, add a little more water. Serve immediately or cover and chill.

Hake Baked in White Wine

This Portuguese dish is usually made with hake, but another firm-fleshed white fish could be substituted.

Serves 4
- 1 lb. potatoes, cut into chunks
- 2 cups mushrooms, quartered or sliced
- 1¼ lb. well-flavored tomatoes, quartered
- 1 onion, chopped
- 1½ lb. hake
- ⅔ cup dry white wine
- 1 tbsp. olive oil
- salt and pepper
- parsley sprigs and lemon slices, to garnish

Method
Preheat the oven to 375°F.

Parboil the potatoes for 5 minutes. Drain and put into an ovenproof dish with the other vegetables. Put the fish on top and pour over the wine and oil. Season and cover with aluminum foil.

Bake for 30–40 minutes until the flesh flakes easily. Serve garnished with parsley sprigs and lemon slices.

Salmon and Pasta Timbales

An Italian dish with a difference!

Serves 4
- ◆ 2 oz. pasta dough (see p.13)
- ◆ salt and pepper
- ◆ 7 oz. can salmon
- ◆ 1 cup fresh white bread crumbs
- ◆ 1 tbsp. finely chopped scallion
- ◆ 3 basil sprigs, finely shredded, or
    1 tbsp. chopped parsley
- ◆ ½ cup Ricotta cheese, strained
- ◆ 1 egg, separated

Garnish
- ◆ basil or parsley sprigs
- ◆ halved lemon slices

Method

Roll out the pasta very thinly. Take a ramekin dish and cut a paper pattern of the base or find a round cutter to fit. Grease and base-line the ramekins with non-stick baking parchment. Cut 12 circles of pasta, then cook them in boiling salted water for 3 minutes. Drain the circles and place a circle of pasta in the bottom of each ramekin. Lay the remaining pasta out on paper towels. Preheat the oven to 350°F.

Drain the salmon, remove any skin and bone, then mash it. Mix with the bread crumbs, scallion, basil or parsley and Ricotta cheese. Add seasoning and beat in the egg yolk. Whisk the egg white until stiff, then fold it into the salmon mixture.

Divide the mixture roughly in half, then spoon one portion into the dishes, dividing it equally between them and spreading it neatly. Top each with a circle of pasta, then divide the remaining mixture between the dishes. Finally, top each with a circle of pasta. Stand on a baking tray, cover with foil and bake for 25–30 minutes, or until the salmon mixture is set. It will also have risen.

Allow to stand for 2 minutes, then slide a knife around the inside of each ramekin. Invert the timbales on individual plates. Remove the non-stick baking parchment. Serve garnished with basil or parsley and lemon.

Above : Salmon and Pasta
Timbales

48

Seafood Lasagne

This is a favorite pasta dish from Italy.

Serves 6

- 12 oz. spinach-flavored pasta dough (see p.13) or fresh lasagne verdi
- 2 tbsp. olive oil
- 2 tbsp. butter
- 1 onion, finely chopped
- 1 bay leaf
- ⅓ cup all-purpose flour
- 1¼ cups dry white wine
- 1¼ cups fish stock
- 1 cup sliced button mushrooms
- salt and pepper
- 1½ lb. white fish fillet, skinned and cut into chunks
- 8 oz. peeled cooked shrimp, thawed if frozen
- 1 lb. mussels, cooked and shelled
- 2 tbsp. chopped parsley
- 1 quantity béchamel sauce (see p.11)
- ½ cup grated Cheddar cheese

Method

Cut the rolled-out pasta into large squares (about 5 inches) or oblong sheets. Lower the pieces of pasta one at a time into a large saucepan of boiling salted water. Bring back to a boil and cook for 3 minutes. Drain and rinse under cold water. Lay the pasta on double-thick sheets of paper towel.

Preheat the oven to 350°F. Heat the oil and butter in a saucepan and add the onion and bay leaf. Cook for 10 minutes, until the onion is softened slightly, then stir in the flour. Slowly pour in the wine and stock and bring to a boil, stirring all the time. Add the mushrooms and seasoning, then simmer for 10 minutes. Remove from the heat before stirring in the fish, shrimp, mussels and parsley. Layer this fish sauce and the lasagne in a large ovenproof dish, ending with a layer of lasagne. Pour the béchamel sauce evenly over the pasta, then sprinkle the cheese on top. Bake for 40–50 minutes, until golden-brown and bubbling hot.

Broiled Scabbard Fish

Most people who have visited Madeira will have come across scabbard fish, the ugly yard-long fish with black and white smudges on its flat body; it is the island's best-known fish. The flesh is white and moist with the texture of sole and a faint flavor of sardines. Tuna, which is also popular on Madeira, can be substituted.

Serves 4
- *4 scabbard or tuna fish steaks*
- *1 garlic clove*
- *small bunch of parsley*
- *juice of 1 large lemon*
- *3 tbsp. olive oil*
- *salt and pepper*

Method
Place the fish in a single layer in a shallow non-metallic dish.

Chop together the garlic and parsley and then mix with the lemon juice, oil, and seasoning. Pour over the fish. Leave in a cool place for about 2 hours, turning the steaks once or twice.

Preheat the broiler. Remove the fish from the marinade and broil for 3–4 minutes on each side, brushing occasionally with the marinade, until the flesh flakes easily when tested with the point of a knife.

Pistachio-fried Fish

In Lebanon, the white fish used for this dish might be grouper (*merou*) or sea bream (*farrideh*). Here sole or bass would do as well.

Serves 6
- ½ cup fine dry bread crumbs
- 1 cup shelled pistachios, finely chopped and crushed
- 3 tbsp. finely chopped flat-leaved parsley
- salt and pepper
- 2 eggs
- 6 × 5-oz. white fish fillets
- ⅓ cup combination of butter and olive oil
- juice of 2 oranges
- toasted chopped pistachios
- orange wedges

Method
On a large plate, mix together the bread crumbs, crushed nuts, parsley and seasoning to taste. Beat the two eggs lightly.

Dip the fish pieces, into the egg. Drain then coat in the nut mixture, patting to ensure an even covering.

Heat half of the butter and oil mixture in a large skillet. Sauté the fillets, 3 at a time, for about 5 minutes on each side, turning once with a spatula. Remove and keep warm while frying the remaining 3 fillets.

Before serving, deglaze the pan with the orange juice. Arrange the fillets on a plate, pour over the pan juices and serve, garnished with toasted pistachios and orange.

Lebanese Tuna Salad

Although fresh tuna is available along the coast of Lebanon, canned tuna is just as popular as a convenience food as it is in the West. This version makes a delicious change from the more unusual Western tuna salads and can serve as a great filling for *khoubz* or pita bread.

Serves 6–8
- 3 medium-sized red bell peppers
- 2 garlic cloves, crushed
- salt and pepper
- 3 tbsp. lemon juice
- ½ cup olive oil
- 1 large red onion, finely chopped
- 2 tbsp. finely chopped cilantro
- ¾ cup pitted black olives, sliced
- 2 hard-cooked eggs, chopped
- 2 × 7-oz. can white tuna in oil or brine
- lemon wedges

Method
Place the peppers under a hot broiler, and cook, until the skins are blackened. Remove, place in a plastic bag and leave for 15 minutes.

Meanwhile, mash the garlic in a large bowl with a little salt until you have a paste. Whisk in the lemon juice and then the olive oil in a slow stream, until the dressing is emulsified. Stir in the onion and cilantro.

Remove the bell peppers from the bag and skin them. Core and seed them, cut away the inner ribs, then cut the flesh into short thin strips. Stir the bell pepper strips into the dressing, cover and chill for 1 hour.

Gently fold in the olives, chopped eggs and flaked tuna. Stir to combine. Transfer the salad to a serving platter and garnish with lemon wedges.

Trout in Tomato Sauce

Wonderfully fresh and tender young trout are to be found in the Serra da Estrela in Portugal. Choose smallish trout that do not have thick skins.

Serves 4

- *1 cup parsley*
- *1 garlic clove, chopped*
- *3 tbsp. olive oil*
- *1¼ lb. well-flavored tomatoes, skinned, seeded, and chopped*
- *½ tsp. tomato paste*
- *salt and pepper*
- *4 trout, about 7 oz.*

Method

Fry the parsley and garlic in the oil in a pan large enough to hold the fish in a single layer, for 1–2 minutes. Stir in the tomatoes and tomato paste and simmer for 5 minutes.

Season the sauce, add the trout and spoon some of the sauce over them to half-cover. Cover and cook gently for about 20 minutes.

Fish Kabobs

Kabobs are one of the most typical dishes of the Lebanon. Those made with fish, however, are usually encountered only along the coast. Kabobs are usually cooked over hot coals, but these fish kabobs work well under a broiler.

Serves 6

- *4 onions, roughly chopped*
- *juice of 3 lemons*
- *¼ cup olive oil*
- *large pinch of cayenne pepper*
- *2 tsp. ground cumin*
- *1 tbsp. tomato paste*
- *2 bay leaves*
- *2 lb. fillet of sea bass, cut into 1-in. cubes*
- *6 baby zucchini, trimmed, scrubbed and cut into 3–4 pieces each*
- *18–24 cherry tomatoes*
- *olive oil*
- *lemon wedges*

Method

Using a garlic press, squeeze the juice from the onion pieces a little at a time, until you have extracted as much as you can. In a bowl, mix the onion juice with the lemon juice and whisk in the oil, cayenne to taste, cumin and tomato paste. Add the bay leaves.

Place the cubed fish in a larger bowl and pour the marinade over it; toss the fish using your hands. Cover and chill for 1 hour.

On 6 large skewers, thread the fish cubes, baby zucchini and cherry tomatoes. Place over hot coals or under a hot broiler, and brush with a little oil. Cook for about 10–15 minutes, turning once or twice, until the fish is opaque and the zucchini are just tender. Serve immediately with lemon wedges and rice or burghul.

Fish in Sesame Sauce

Tahini (sesame seed) paste can be bought at most delicatessens. The sesame sauce used in this recipe is usually baked with fish or cauliflower.

Serves 6
- ◆ 1½ cups sesame sauce (see below)
- ◆ ½ cup olive oil
- ◆ 2 large onions, thinly sliced
- ◆ 6 white fish fillets (brill, sea bass, or suchlike)
- ◆ salt and pepper

Method

Make the sauce first, and set it aside.

Heat the olive oil in a skillet. Add the onions and sauté, stirring frequently, until they are limp and lightly golden.

Preheat the oven to 350°F. Transfer the onions to a large baking dish. Roll each of the fillets in the onions to coat with the oil, then arrange the fish on top of the onions, skin side up. Season to taste, cover with foil and bake for 15 minutes. Remove, and if desired, pass the fish under a hot broiler for a few minutes to crisp the skin.

Spoon the sauce over the fish and onions. Return the fish to the oven at the same temperature and bake, uncovered, for a further 20–25 minutes, or until the sauce is bubbling. Serve with pilau rice.

Sesame Sauce

This is the most frequently encountered of Lebanese sauces. It is served hot or cold with both fish and vegetables.

Makes about 1½ cups
- ◆ 2 garlic cloves, crushed
- ◆ ¾ tsp. salt
- ◆ large pinch of cayenne pepper
- ◆ 1 cup tahini paste
- ◆ ½ cup lemon juice

Method

In a bowl, mash the garlic together with the salt and cayenne until it makes a paste. Whisk in the tahini with a fork, then thin the mixture with the lemon juice, beating continuously. Serve the sauce immediately or cover and chill.

The sauce can be kept refrigerated for 2 weeks, and it can also be frozen.

Squid with Bell Peppers and Tomato

A Portuguese way of cooking squid, seafood that features in many Mediterranean dishes. Cook the squid gently so that it is not irrevocably toughened.

Serves 4

- ◆ 2¼ lb. squid, prepared
- ◆ ½ cup olive oil
- ◆ 2 onions, finely chopped
- ◆ 1 garlic clove, crushed
- ◆ 2 red bell peppers, cored, seeded, and sliced
- ◆ 1 lb. well-flavored tomatoes, chopped
- ◆ 1 cup fish stock
- ◆ 6 tbsp. dry white wine
- ◆ salt and pepper
- ◆ 2 slices country bread, toasted
- ◆ 1 tbsp. chopped parsley

Method

Cut the squid open into two halves, then cut across into 1-inch slices.

Heat the oil in a flameproof casserole. Add the onions, garlic, and bell peppers, and cook until softened. Stir in the tomatoes and bubble until well-blended and lightly thickened. Add the stock and wine, bring to a boil and then lower the heat. Add the squid and seasoning, cover and cook gently for 1–1½ hours, or until the squid is tender and the cooking juices have reduced to a light sauce; if necessary, remove the lid towards the end of cooking to allow the sauce to evaporate slightly.

Toast the bread, cut the slices in half and put into a warmed, deep serving dish. Pour over the squid mixture and sprinkle with parsley.

Piquant Shrimp and Tomato Sauce

Good with spaghetti or noodles, this Italian sauce may also be layered with lasagne, then covered with a creamy topping and baked.

Serves 4

- ◆ 2 tbsp. oil
- ◆ 2 garlic cloves, crushed
- ◆ 2 green chilis, seeded and chopped
- ◆ 1 large onion, chopped
- ◆ 1 green bell pepper, seeded and diced
- ◆ 1 carrot, diced
- ◆ 2 celery stalks, diced
- ◆ 1 bay leaf
- ◆ 2 × 14 oz. cans chopped tomatoes
- ◆ 1 tbsp. tomato paste
- ◆ 1 tsp. sugar
- ◆ salt and pepper
- ◆ 1 lb. frozen peeled cooked shrimp
- ◆ 2 tbsp. chopped cilantro

Method

Heat the oil in a large saucepan. Add the garlic, chilis, onion, green bell pepper, carrot, celery and bay leaf. Cook, stirring, for 20 minutes. Then stir in the tomatoes, tomato paste, sugar and plenty of seasoning. Bring to a boil, reduce the heat, cover and simmer gently for 30 minutes.

Add the shrimp, stir well and cook for 15 minutes, or until they are hot through. Taste for seasoning, then ladle the sauce over the pasta and top with the cilantro.

Right : Squid with Bell Peppers and Tomato

Baked Fish

This common Western method of baking fish has been adopted by the Lebanese with enthusiasm, since it suits much of the typical Mediterranean catch, allows spices to be rubbed into the fish, and is admirably suited to fish that are to be served cold.

Serves 4–6

◆ *1 garlic clove, crushed*
◆ *juice of ½ lemon*
◆ *½ cup olive oil*
◆ *2 tsp. oregano*
◆ *salt and pepper*
◆ *1 whole sea bass, or 2–3 whole red mullet, depending on size*
◆ *lemon wedges (optional)*

Method

In a small bowl, mash the garlic into the lemon juice until you have a paste. Whisk in the olive oil until emulsified, then the oregano and seasoning to taste.

Place the fish on a large piece of foil and pour some of the marinade over it. Rub it into the fish on both sides. Close the foil over the fish, and chill for 1–2 hours.

Preheat the oven to 350°F. Open the foil, pour over a little more marinade, and seal again. Place on a baking sheet and cook for 40–50 minutes. Test by inserting a knife into the flesh; it should be opaque.

Serve hot with lemon wedges, or cold – with the skin removed – with Cardamom Fish Sauce (below).

Fish in a Cardamom Sauce

Lemon and cilantro pep up plain white fish in this delicious pasta sauce. It is particularly good with spirals or small pieces of pasta, such as squares or cut-up spaghetti; saffron or turmeric pasta is ideal if you are making your own.

Serves 4

◆ *2 tbsp. butter*
◆ *1 small onion, finely chopped*
◆ *1 red bell pepper, seeded and diced*
◆ *6 green cardamoms*
◆ *1 bay leaf*
◆ *grated zest of 1 lemon*
◆ *¼ cup all-purpose flour*
◆ *1¼ cups fish stock*
◆ *salt and pepper*
◆ *1½ lb. white fish fillet, skinned and cut into chunks*
◆ *1¼ cups light cream*
◆ *2 tbsp. chopped cilantro*

Method

Melt the butter in a saucepan. Add the onion, bell pepper, cardamoms, bay leaf and lemon zest. Press the cardamoms to split them slightly, then cook gently for 20 minutes, until the onion and bell pepper are well cooked. Stir often, so that the bay and spices give up their flavor and the onions do not brown.

Stir in the flour, then gradually pour in the stock, stirring all the time, and bring to a boil. Reduce the heat, if necessary, so that the sauce just simmers – it will be too thick at this stage. Add seasoning and the fish. Stir lightly, then cover the pan and cook gently for 20 minutes, or until the fish is cooked. Gently stir in the cream, then heat through without boiling. Taste for seasoning before serving sprinkled with the cilantro.

Seafood Medley

You can vary the mixture of seafood in this Italian dish according to your budget, the choice at the fish vendors and personal preference. Remember to add delicate ingredients at the end so they do not over-cook. Serve with plain pasta or try combining a mixture of tomato, spinach and plain pasta.

Serves 4

- ◆ *2 lb. mussels*
- ◆ *1 bay leaf*
- ◆ *1¼ cups dry white wine*
- ◆ *6 tbsp. olive oil*
- ◆ *1 onion, halved and thinly sliced*
- ◆ *1 celery stalk, finely diced*
- ◆ *1 green bell pepper, seeded and finely diced*
- ◆ *3 garlic cloves, crushed*
- ◆ *grated zest of 1 lemon*
- ◆ *salt and pepper*
- ◆ *4 small squid, cleaned and sliced*
- ◆ *12 oz. monkfish fillet, cut into small chunks*
- ◆ *6–8 scallops, shelled and sliced*
- ◆ *12 oz. peeled cooked shrimp, thawed if frozen*
- ◆ *8 black olives, pitted and chopped*
- ◆ *plenty of chopped parsley*
- ◆ *freshly grated Parmesan cheese, to serve*

Method

Scrub the mussels and scrape off any barnacles or dirt on the shell. Pull away the black beard which protrudes from the shell. Discard any open mussels which do not shut when tapped. Place the mussels in a large pan and add the bay leaf and wine. Bring the wine to a boil, then put a close-fitting lid on the pan and reduce the heat slightly so that the wine does not boil too rapidly. Cook for about 10 minutes, shaking the pan often, until the mussels are all open. Discard any that do not open. Strain the mussels, reserving the cooking liquor and bay leaf. Reserve a few mussels in shells for garnish, if you like, and use a fork to remove the others from their shells.

Heat the oil in a large saucepan. Add the reserved bay leaf, onion, celery, green bell pepper, garlic, lemon zest and plenty of seasoning. Cover and cook, stirring occasionally, for 20 minutes, or until the onion is softened but not browned. Pour in the liquor from the mussels, bring to a boil and boil hard for about 3 minutes, or until reduced by half. Then reduce the heat and add the squid. Cover the pan and simmer for 5 minutes. Add the monkfish, cover the pan again and cook for a further 5 minutes. Next, add the scallops and cook gently for 3 minutes, or until the seafood is just cooked.

Add the shrimp, mussels and olives. Heat gently, then taste for seasoning. Stir in plenty of parsley and serve at once, with Parmesan cheese to sprinkle over the seafood and pasta.

COOK'S TIP

To clean squid, first wash it. Pull the head and tentacles from the body sac. Cut the tentacles off just above the head and slice them if you want to add them to the dish. Discard the other head parts and innards. Pull out the transparent quill which is inside the body sac, then rinse the sac well. Rub off the spotted skin to leave the squid clean and white. The flaps may rub off and these can be sliced separately. Slice the sac in thin rings.

Fish Fillets with Tomato Sauce

Fillets of white fish, such as whiting and sole or flounder, are particularly popular in the Arrabida area and in Lisbon. A favorite Portuguese way of serving them is accompanied by a tomato sauce.

Serves 4
- ◆ 5 tbsp. butter
- ◆ 1 onion, finely chopped
- ◆ 1 garlic clove, crushed
- ◆ 1¼ lb. tomatoes, skinned, seeded, and chopped
- ◆ ½ cup fish stock (see p.11)
- ◆ ½ cup dry white wine
- ◆ 1 tbsp. chopped parsley
- ◆ 1½ lb. white fish fillets
- ◆ salt and pepper

Method

Melt 2 tablespoons of the butter in a saucepan and cook the onion and garlic until softened. Add the tomatoes, half the stock and half the wine, and the parsley. Simmer, stirring occasionally, until thickened to a well-blended sauce.

Meanwhile, lay the fish fillets in a large skillet and add the remaining stock and wine, 1 tablespoon of the butter, and seasoning. Bring to simmering point; then poach gently until the flesh flakes when tested with the point of a knife.

Transfer the fish to a warmed serving plate and keep warm. Pour the juices from the skillet into the tomato sauce, add the remaining butter and boil to a sauce consistency. Season and pour around the fish.

Baked Sardines

In Portugal, a popular way of cooking sardines is over charcoal. When this is not convenient, or simply for a change, the fish are often baked with tomatoes and herbs.

Serves 4
- ◆ 2¼ lb. fresh sardines, scaled, gutted, and heads removed
- ◆ salt and pepper
- ◆ 1 tbsp. olive oil
- ◆ 1¼ cups tomatoes, skinned, seeded, and diced
- ◆ 1 garlic clove, finely chopped
- ◆ 1 small onion, finely chopped
- ◆ leaves from a bunch of both parsley and dill, chopped
- ◆ scant 1 cup dry white wine

Method

Preheat the oven to 350°F.

Season the fish and brush with half the oil. Use the remaining oil to grease a shallow baking dish.

Mix together the tomatoes, garlic, onion, herbs, wine, and seasoning, and spread over the bottom of the dish. Put the sardines on top, pushing them into the tomato mixture. Bake for 5–6 minutes.

Left : Fish Fillets with Tomato Sauce

CHAPTER 3

POULTRY AND EGGS

····

THIS CHAPTER OFFERS A RANGE OF DISHES FROM A

SIMPLE CHARCOAL-GRILLED CHICKEN FROM

PORTUGAL TO MORE ELABORATE RECIPES SUCH AS

MUSCAT-BAKED ALMOND CHICKEN FROM THE

LEBANON. IF YOU CAN OBTAIN FREE-RANGE POULTRY

WITH A GOOD NATURAL FLAVOR YOU NEED GO TO

LITTLE TROUBLE TO CREATE A DELICIOUS MEAL; A

FROZEN MASS-PRODUCED BIRD WILL REQUIRE A BIT

MORE JAZZING UP FOR A REALLY GOOD RESULT.

Chicken Piri-piri

Piri-piri sauce makes an appearance in many Portuguese dishes. Take care when adding it as it can be very hot; the strength of the homemade sauce will depend on the fieriness of the chilis you have used. If you do not have any homemade Piri-piri it is possible to buy it from specialist Portuguese food stores, or hot pepper sauce can be substituted.

Serves 6
- *oil for frying*
- *6 chicken portions*
- *2 onions, sliced into rings*
- *6 tomatoes, chopped*
- *2 carrots, cut into sticks*
- *1 large parsnip, cut into sticks*
- *1 cinnamon stick*
- *salt and pepper*
- *Piri-piri (see below)*
- *1 large red bell pepper, cored, seeded, and thinly sliced*
- *1 large yellow bell pepper, cored, seeded, and thinly sliced*

Method
Heat the oil in a large flameproof casserole. Add the chicken portions, in batches if necessary, and brown evenly. Add the onions, tomatoes, carrots, parsnip, cinnamon, seasoning, and 3 cups water.

Bring the contents of the casserole to a boil, stir in a little Piri-piri, cover and simmer gently for 30 minutes.

Add the bell peppers to the casserole, cover again and continue to simmer gently for 30 minutes, or until the chicken and vegetables are tender.

Using a slotted spoon, transfer the chicken and vegetables to a warmed serving dish. Keep warm.

Boil the cooking liquid rapidly until reduced by about a third. Taste and add more Piri-piri if necessary. Pour the sauce over the chicken and vegetables and serve.

Piri-piri Sauce

This is a chili-based sauce that provides the fire in many savory dishes – it is easier to add a few drops of the ready-made chili-based sauce than to seed and chop chilis each time. Like other traditional recipes, nearly everyone who makes Piri-piri has their own version, the simplest of which is to fill a third of a jar or bottle with small, hot red chilis, then top up with olive oil, cover and leave in a cool place for at least 1 month so the oil is impregnated with the heat of the chilis. Other versions, like this one, include lemon juice or vinegar.

Makes about 5 tablespoons
- *½ small red bell pepper, seeded and sliced*
- *4–5 fresh red chilis, seeded and sliced*
- *juice of 1½ lemons*
- *2 tsp. olive oil*
- *salt*

Method
Simmer the red bell pepper and chilis in a saucepan with the lemon juice for about 15 minutes until tender.

Mix to a thick paste with the oil in a blender. Season with salt. Pour into a small bottle or jar, cover and keep in a cool place.

Chicken Baked with Potatoes and Garlic

An extremely easy Portuguese dish to make and cook, and based on simple ingredients. It is also delicious to eat, provided that good potatoes and a fresh free-range chicken are used, as they would be in Portugal. Don't be put off by the amount of garlic – the flavor mellows to a mild creaminess during the cooking.

Serves 6
◆ 3½ lb. chicken, cut into 12–16 pieces
◆ 2¼ lb. yellow waxy potatoes, quartered
◆ 1 onion, sliced
◆ 20 small-medium sprigs of rosemary
◆ salt and pepper
◆ 8 tbsp. olive oil
◆ 20 unpeeled garlic cloves

Method
Preheat the oven to 425°F. Put the chicken, potatoes, onion, rosemary, and seasoning into a large, shallow baking dish. Mix together and pour over the oil. Scatter the garlic cloves over the top and bake for 20 minutes.

Lower the oven temperature to 375°F and bake for about 45 minutes, turning the chicken and potatoes occasionally, until the chicken is cooked, the potatoes golden and the garlic crisp.

Right : Chicken Baked with Potatoes and Garlic

Lebanese Stuffed Chicken

Stuffed poultry is a favorite all over the Arab world, from Morocco – where stuffing is made with couscous, cinnamon and pickled lemon pieces – to Lebanon, where the staple ingredient varies between burghul and rice, both of which are usually enriched with nuts and herbs.

Serves 6
- 4 tbsp. butter
- 8 oz. ground lamb
- 1 large onion, finely chopped
- 2 tbsp. pine nuts
- 1 tbsp. raisins
- 1⅓ cups long-grain rice
- salt and pepper
- 1 tbsp. honey
- 3 tbsp. Greek-style yogurt
- 4½ lb. free-range roasting chicken

Method

Heat 1 tablespoon of butter in a skillet. Gently sauté the ground lamb, stirring to ensure it browns all over. Transfer the meat with a slotted spoon to a plate, add another 1 tablespoon butter to the pan and stir in the finely chopped onion. Sauté over medium-low heat for about 5 minutes, until it is limp; add the pine nuts and continue to sauté until both onions and nuts are lightly colored. Add the raisins and rice, and stir for a minute or two until the rice is transparent; season to taste. Pour in 2 cups water and bring to a boil. Reduce the heat, cover and simmer for about 25 minutes, or until the rice has absorbed all the water. Leave until it is cool enough to handle.

Preheat the oven to 400°F. Melt the remaining butter in a saucepan, take off the heat; stir in the honey until it melts, then the yogurt. Stuff the chicken with the rice mixture, and secure the opening with skewers. Leave the remaining rice in the pan to be warmed up later. Place the chicken in a roasting pan and baste generously with the yogurt sauce.

Roast for 20 minutes at the above temperature, then reduce the heat to 350°F for a further 1¼–1½ hours. Baste twice with the yogurt sauce. Test to see if the chicken is cooked by piercing the joint between body and thigh with a skewer; the juice should run clear.

Heat the remaining rice gently over low heat, moistened with a little of the chicken pan juices. Serve with the hot stuffed chicken.

Garlic Chicken on a Stick

A Greek dish that takes just minutes to prepare. A handy tip is to soak the wooden skewers in lemon juice for 30 minutes before using them. This gives a tangy flavor to the chicken and helps to prevent the sticks from burning under the broiler.

Serves 6

- ◆ *6 chicken breast halves, skinned and boned*
- ◆ *6 garlic cloves, crushed*
- ◆ *salt and pepper*
- ◆ *juice of 2 lemons*
- ◆ *¼ cup olive oil*
- ◆ *6 tbsp. very finely chopped fresh parsley*

Method

Cut the chicken halves into 1-inch pieces and place in a shallow dish.

In a small bowl, mix together the garlic, salt and pepper, lemon juice and olive oil. Pour the marinade over the chicken pieces, stir, cover and marinate for 2–4 hours in the refrigerator, turning occasionally.

Spread the parsley out on a plate. Divide the chicken pieces into six equal portions and thread onto six wooden skewers. Roll each skewer in the parsley to coat evenly.

Arrange the chicken skewers on an oiled broiler rack and cook for 5–10 minutes or until the chicken is golden on the outside and cooked through. Turn and rearrange the skewers, basting them with the remaining marinade during cooking for an even more delicious result.

Chicken with Apricots and Olives

Although it is a Lebanese dish, this savory combination owes more to the Israeli taste than to classic Lebanese cuisine. Israel is Europe's richest source of dried fruits, and they make a frequent appearance in the meat stews and desserts of that country. However, taste cannot be confined by national borders, and dishes like this one have become common in Lebanon, adapted to include specialties such as arak.

Serves 8

- 3½ lb. skinned, boned and cubed chicken
- 5 garlic cloves, crushed
- ¾ cup chopped ready-to-eat dried apricots
- ½ cup black Greek olives
- ½ tsp. grated orange zest
- 5 tbsp. orange juice
- 2 tbsp. lemon juice or white wine vinegar
- ½ cup arak (anise-based Lebanese liqueur) or ouzo
- 2 tbsp. fresh fennel leaves
- 1½ tbsp. olive oil
- ¾ cup light brown sugar

Method

Preheat the oven to 400°F. Combine all the ingredients except the sugar in a large bowl and stir carefully to mix well. Cover and chill overnight.

Transfer the chicken pieces to a baking pan and pour over the marinade, including the olives and apricots. Sprinkle over the sugar. Bake for about 30 minutes, turning once or twice.

Remove the chicken pieces to a serving platter, and arrange the olives and apricots over and around them. Strain the cooking juices into a saucepan, and reduce over high heat to about half. Pour the sauce over the chicken. Serve warm or cold.

Chicken in Blue

In this Italian recipe, blue cheese makes a rich sauce for chicken. Serve large quantities of plain fresh pasta noodles to balance the full flavor of the sauce. Here Danish blue is used but any other blue cheese may be substituted – Dolcelatte, for example, or tangy Gorgonzola for a really powerful flavor.

Serves 4
- ◆ 2 tbsp. olive oil
- ◆ 1 garlic clove, crushed
- ◆ 1 red bell pepper, seeded and diced
- ◆ 2½ cups skinned, boneless, diced chicken
- ◆ salt and pepper
- ◆ 2 cups small button mushrooms
- ◆ 4 tbsp. dry white wine
- ◆ ⅝ cup light cream
- ◆ 8 oz. Danish blue cheese, cut into small pieces
- ◆ 2 scallions, finely chopped
- ◆ 2 tbsp. chopped parsley

Method
Heat the oil in a large skillet. Add the garlic, red bell pepper and chicken with some seasoning – go easy on the salt at this stage as the blue cheese can make the sauce quite salty. Cook, stirring often, for about 20 minutes, or until the diced chicken is lightly browned and cooked.

Add the mushrooms and cook for 2 minutes, then pour in the wine and bring to a boil. Turn the heat to the lowest setting and make sure the mixture has stopped boiling before pouring in the cream and stirring in the cheese. Stir over low heat until the cheese has melted. Do not allow the sauce to simmer or it will curdle.

When the cheese has melted, taste the sauce, then pour it over the pasta and sprinkle with scallions and parsley. Serve at once.

Lemon Chicken

Chicken flavored with lemon is such a delicious combination of tastes and one that is commonly found in Greece. There is plenty of sauce in this dish so rice is a welcome accompaniment.

Serves 6–8

- ¼ cup butter
- 3½ lb. prepared chicken, without giblets, cut into small portions
- salt and pepper
- 1¼ cups boiling water
- 1 bunch scallions, trimmed and cut into 1-in. pieces
- 3 eggs
- 3 tbsp. lemon juice
- 2 tbsp. chopped fresh dill, to garnish

Method

Melt the butter in a large, heavy-based saucepan and add the chicken. Cook for about 5 minutes, or until evenly browned.

Season the chicken with salt and pepper and add the boiling water and the scallions. Cover and simmer for 35–40 minutes, until the chicken is tender and cooked through.

Place the eggs in a small bowl and beat well. Gradually whisk in the lemon juice, a little at a time to prevent curdling. Whisk in 1¼ cups of the cooking liquid from the chicken. Pour the egg and lemon mixture over the chicken and stir continuously until the sauce has thickened slightly. Do not boil.

Transfer the chicken and sauce to a warm dish and sprinkle with the fresh dill.

Chicken and Tomato Casserole

A Greek dish in which the chicken is cooked in a rich tomato sauce.

Serves 4–6

- ¼ *cup olive oil*
- *3½ lb. chicken, cut into portions*
- *flour for dredging*
- *2 large red onions, sliced*
- *2 × 15-oz. cans chopped tomatoes*
- *3 garlic cloves, crushed*
- *salt and pepper*
- *6 tbsp. boiling water*
- *2 tbsp. red wine vinegar*
- *chopped fresh parsley, to garnish*

Method

Preheat the oven to 375°F. Heat the oil in a large, flameproof casserole. Place the chicken portions on a chopping board and dredge all over with flour. Place in the casserole and cook for about 5 minutes, or until evenly browned, turning the portions as they cook. Using a slotted spoon, transfer the chicken portions to a plate and set aside.

Add the onion to the casserole and cook for 3 minutes, or until softened. Return the chicken to the casserole, add the chopped tomatoes and garlic and season with salt and pepper. Add the boiling water, cover, and cook in the oven for 45–55 minutes or until the chicken is tender and the sauce has thickened.

In the last 5 minutes of cooking time, stir in the red wine vinegar and a little extra boiling water if necessary. Serve sprinkled with chopped fresh parsley.

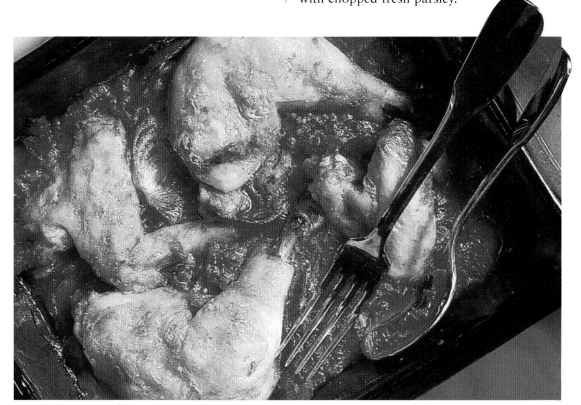

Rice with Chicken

Vibrant green paddy fields can still be seen in the lagoons along the west coast of Portugal. Adding rice is a good way of making meat go further.

Serves 4
- 1 large onion, chopped
- 4 tbsp. olive oil
- 2 garlic cloves, finely chopped
- 1–2 fresh red chilis, seeded and chopped
- 1 red bell pepper, cored, seeded, and chopped
- 4 boneless half chicken breasts, skinned and cut into thin strips
- 1⅔ cups long-grain rice
- 2½ cups chicken stock
- ½ cup medium-bodied dry white wine, or additional stock
- salt and pepper
- 8 oz. chouriço, cut into thick slices
- ⅔ cup frozen peas
- 10 oil-cured black olives, pitted and sliced
- 2 tbsp. chopped parsley

Method

Cook the onion in the oil in a large flameproof casserole until softened. Add the garlic, chilis, red bell pepper, and chicken, and cook gently for 2–3 minutes.

Add the rice, stock, wine, and seasoning. Bring to a boil, then cover and simmer for 12 minutes.

Stir in the chouriço, peas, olives, and parsley until just mixed, then cover the casserole and cook for a further 6 minutes or until the liquid has been absorbed and the rice is tender.

Fluff up with a fork and serve immediately.

Chicken Wings with Lime Juice and Garlic

Whenever you buy a whole chicken, freeze the wings if they are not needed. When you have enough collected in the freezer you can transform them into this deliciously tangy recipe.

Serves 8–12
- ◆ *12 chicken wings*
- ◆ *4 garlic cloves, crushed*
- ◆ *salt and pepper*
- ◆ *juice of 4 limes*
- ◆ *pinch of cayenne pepper*

Method

Place the chicken wings in a shallow dish. Rub the crushed garlic all over the chicken wings, then season with salt and pepper.

Sprinkle the lime juice and cayenne pepper over the chicken wings, cover, and marinate in the refrigerator for 3–4 hours, turning and rearranging them occasionally.

Arrange the chicken wings in a large skillet and pour the marinade over them. Add just enough cold water to cover the wings and bring quickly to a boil. Cook, uncovered, for 20–25 minutes, or until the chicken is cooked through and the sauce has reduced slightly. Serve warm or, better still, cold the next day.

Muscat Baked Almond Chicken

This Lebanese dish is made with the sweet white-green grapes that have been grown around Cyprus and the Levant since Crusader times. Both a wine-making and a dessert grape, the muscat gives a pungent flavor and aroma to this recipe, which has its roots in a centuries-old tradition of using ground almonds as a thickening agent. In Lebanon, the herbs used would be wild – the marjoram, in particular, of a type found only in the eastern Mediterranean.

Serves 6

- 4½ lb. free-range chicken
- salt and pepper
- ½ tsp. cinnamon
- large pinch of mace
- fresh lemon thyme
- fresh marjoram
- 3 cups muscat grapes, peeled, seeded and halved
- 1 cup sweet muscat wine
- 1 tbsp. butter
- 3 tbsp. sliced blanched almonds
- ½ cup ground almonds
- ½ cup light cream
- 2 egg yolks

Method

Preheat the oven to 400°F. Wash and pat dry the chicken, rub it all over with salt and pepper to taste, the cinnamon and the mace. Take 2–3 sprigs of lemon thyme and the same of marjoram and put them inside the chicken. Place it in a casserole, stuff with half the grapes and pour over the wine. Cover and cook the chicken in the oven for 1½ hours.

Remove the chicken from the oven and transfer it to a warm serving platter. Remove the grapes and herbs from the cavity, cut the chicken into portions and cover it with foil to keep it warm.

In a small saucepan, melt the butter and sauté the sliced almonds for a few minutes until just colored. Remove with a slotted spoon and set aside. Skim the fat from the chicken cooking juices in the casserole and strain them into the saucepan. Heat the juices gently until very hot, but not boiling, and stir in the remaining grapes and the ground almonds. Allow to cook for a few minutes to combine.

In a small bowl beat the cream and egg yolks together lightly. Take a spoonful of the hot chicken stock and stir it into the egg. Remove the saucepan from the heat and stir in the egg mixture; the sauce should thicken as you stir.

Pour some of the sauce over the chicken portions and sprinkle it with the toasted almonds. Pour the remainder into a sauceboat to be served with pilau rice.

Chicken Oregano

This simple, tasty Greek dish is perfect for the barbecue on a hot summer's day, or broiled for a fast meze dish.

Serves 6–8
- 6–8 chicken portions
- ½ cup olive oil
- ½ cup dry white wine
- 2 tbsp. dried oregano
- salt and pepper
- 2 garlic cloves, crushed

Method
Arrange the chicken portions in a large, shallow dish.

In a small bowl, combine the oil, wine, oregano, salt and pepper and the garlic. Mix well. Spread the marinade over the chicken portions, cover, and marinate for 2–3 hours, turning and rearranging occasionally.

Place the chicken portions on an oiled broiler rack and cook under a preheated broiler for about 30 minutes or until the chicken is crisp and golden on the outside and cooked through, turning and rearranging several times during cooking. Serve warm or cold.

Charcoal-grilled Chicken

In Portugal, food cooked over charcoal is always in demand, especially in the open air and in the south, not only for the delicious flavor it acquires during cooking, but also because of the informal, convivial atmosphere associated with it.

Serves 4
- ◆ 1 garlic clove, crushed
- ◆ 5 tbsp. dry white wine
- ◆ about ½ tsp. paprika
- ◆ Piri-piri (see p.64) or hot pepper sauce
- ◆ salt and pepper
- ◆ 4 chicken portions

Method
Mix the garlic and wine with paprika, Piri-piri or hot pepper sauce, and seasoning to taste.

Slash each chicken portion three times and arrange in a single layer in a shallow dish. Spoon over the wine mixture, rubbing it in well. Cover and leave in a cool place for 2 hours, turning occasionally.

Preheat a barbecue or broiler. Remove the chicken from the dish and cook on the barbecue or broiler for about 25 minutes until the juices run clear, turning twice and basting with any remaining wine mixture.

Chicken with Feta and Green Olives

This dish originates from a small village called Barthouna, near Sparta, Greece. It is either prepared with olives or raisins, both being major products of this region.

Serves 4
- ◆ *4 chicken breast halves*
- ◆ *flour for dredging*
- ◆ *salt and pepper*
- ◆ *6 tbsp. olive oil*
- ◆ *12 oz. pear onions (or use large onions, quartered)*
- ◆ *15 oz. can chopped tomatoes*
- ◆ *½ cup boiling water*
- ◆ *10 oz. pitted green olives, washed and drained*
- ◆ *1 tbsp. red wine vinegar*
- ◆ *4 oz. Feta cheese, sliced thinly*

Method
Dredge the chicken with the flour and season with salt and pepper on both sides.

Heat the oil in a large, deep skillet and add the chicken portions, skin-sides down. Cook on both sides for 3–5 minutes or until browned. Lift the chicken portions out of the pan and set aside.

Add the onions to the skillet and sauté for about 5 minutes or until softened. Return the chicken to the pan and add the chopped tomatoes and boiling water. Season with salt and pepper, cover, and simmer for 25–30 minutes or until the chicken is tender and cooked through. Add extra boiling water if necessary.

In the last 10 minutes of the cooking time, add the green olives and red wine vinegar. Stir to combine. Place a slice of Feta cheese on top of each piece of chicken and continue to cook, uncovered, for a further 10 minutes, or until the cheese has just melted. Serve immediately.

Chicken Roasted with Pistachios

This is a variation of one of Greece's most popular dishes. The chicken should be cut up into pieces and served with the stuffing separately at the meze table.

Serves 6–8

- ¼ cup olive oil
- 2 onions, finely chopped
- 1⅓ cups long-grain rice
- 4 large tomatoes, peeled, seeded and chopped
- 1⅓ cups shelled pistachio nuts, roughly chopped
- ⅔ cup seedless raisins
- pinch of ground cinnamon
- salt and pepper
- 2¼ cups boiling water
- 3 tbsp. very finely chopped fresh parsley
- 3½ lb. chicken
- ¼ cup dry white wine

Method

Preheat the oven to 450°F. Heat half of the olive oil in a large, heavy skillet and sauté the onion for about 5 minutes or until softened.

Add the rice to the skillet and continue to cook for a further 3 minutes or until the rice begins to brown, stirring occasionally. Add half of the tomatoes, the pistachios, raisins, cinnamon, salt and pepper and ¾ cup boiling water. Simmer for about 10 minutes or until the liquid is mostly absorbed and the rice is almost cooked, stirring continuously. Remove from the heat and stir in the parsley.

Spoon the rice mixture into the cavity of the chicken without packing it too firmly. Place the chicken in a roasting pan and spoon any remaining rice mixture around the outside. Season the chicken with salt and pepper.

Scatter the remaining chopped tomatoes around the chicken and pour 1½ cups boiling water and the wine into the pan. Reduce the oven temperature to 350°F. In this way the chicken skin is seared and made crispy before the oven adjusts to the lower heat. Drizzle the remaining olive oil over the chicken and roast for about 1½ hours or until the chicken is cooked through and the rice, inside and outside of the chicken, is tender. The chicken should be basted several times during cooking and a little extra water may be added if necessary. Allow the chicken to stand for 10 minutes before cutting into portions and serving with the stuffing.

Braised Duck with Sweet Potatoes

Live ducks as well as chickens are a common sight of Lebanese street markets, and in smaller towns such feathered livestock will be found wandering the back roads around peasant houses. The sweet potato is an introduction from Central Africa, which has been accepted into the regional cuisine and into this Maronite recipe.

Serves 6

- ◆ *6 duck quarters, washed and patted dry*
- ◆ *salt and pepper*
- ◆ *2 carrots, chopped*
- ◆ *2 celery stalks, chopped*
- ◆ *1 large onion, chopped*
- ◆ *1 garlic clove, crushed*
- ◆ *1 bay leaf*
- ◆ *1 tsp. thyme*
- ◆ *6 cardamom pods*
- ◆ *1 tbsp. tomato paste*
- ◆ *2 cups duck or chicken consommé*
- ◆ *4 medium sweet potatoes, peeled and roughly cubed*
- ◆ *1 tbsp. olive oil*
- ◆ *2 tbsp. superfine sugar*
- ◆ *4 tbsp. red wine vinegar*
- ◆ *1 tbsp. honey*
- ◆ *2 tbsp. white raisins*

Method

Trim the duck of all extra skin and fat. Place the trimmings in a large shallow casserole, together with the duck quarters, seasoned with salt and pepper, and fry for about 20 minutes, until the trimmings are frizzled and the duck quarters are crisp and brown. Discard the trimmings, reserve the duck quarters, and strain the fat into a heavy saucepan.

Sauté the carrots, celery and onion in the saucepan for about 8 minutes, stirring until they are colored and the onion is limp. Pour off the fat, stir in the garlic briefly over the heat, and add the bay leaf, thyme, cardamom, tomato paste, consommé and 1 cup water. Stir to combine, bring to a boil, lower the heat slightly and simmer for 30 minutes, skimming once or twice.

Preheat the oven to 350°F. Place the duck back in the casserole, strain over the stock, cover and cook for about 40 minutes.

Meanwhile, put the sweet potatoes into the saucepan. Cover with water and bring to a boil. Cook for 5 minutes, then drain.

When the duck is cooked, remove the pieces from the casserole and strain off the juice into a bowl. Add the olive oil to the casserole and sauté the sweet potatoes, for about 5 minutes. Add the duck and remove from the heat.

Skim the fat from the reserved duck stock. In a saucepan, cook the sugar and vinegar together, stirring until the mixture is beginning to caramelize. Whisk in the duck stock and honey until smooth.

Pour the sweet-sour sauce over the sweet potatoes and duck quarters, add the raisins, and cover the casserole. Simmer for about 10 minutes. Serve immediately.

Braised Partridge

The beach at Guincho, northwest of Lisbon, Portugal, is a weekend playground for Lisboans in summer, but in the fall men in particular turn their attention to the heath behind the beach to indulge their love of shooting.

Serves 4
- *4 dressed partridge*
- *salt and pepper*
- *olive oil*
- *2 Savoy cabbages, halved*
- *8 oz. piece presunto or lightly smoked bacon, cut into strips*
- *1 large onion, chopped*
- *¼ cup diced carrots*
- *2 celery stalks, diced*
- *6 juniper berries*
- *1¼ cups game or chicken stock*

Method

Preheat the oven to 400°F. Season the partridge inside and out and brush liberally with oil. Roast the birds for 14–16 minutes, first on one side, then on the other, turning halfway through. Meanwhile, cut the core from the cabbages and coarsely shred the leaves.

Heat a little oil in a deep, heavy-based flameproof casserole. Add the presunto or bacon and cook over a medium heat, stirring, for 3 minutes. Stir in the onion, carrots, and celery, and cook for a further 3 minutes until they begin to color. Then add the cabbage. Lower the heat, cover the casserole and cook for 5 minutes. Stir in the juniper berries and pepper, cover again and cook for a further 5 minutes. Push the partridge, breast-sides up, down into the cabbage so they are half-buried. Pour over the stock, cover the birds with oiled foil and return to the oven for about 25 minutes.

Left : Braised Duck with Sweet Potatoes

Pasta with Eggs and Tarragon

An easy Italian dish that makes a tasty change from poached eggs on toast! Serve half portions for a starter or light snack.

Serves 4

◆ ⅓ cup butter (or use olive oil or a mixture of butter and olive oil if preferred)
◆ 3 tbsp. chopped tarragon
◆ 8 eggs
◆ 1 lb. tagliatelle
◆ plenty of chopped fresh parsley
◆ freshly grated Parmesan cheese, to serve

Method
Warm four plates or bowls. Melt the butter (or heat the oil with the butter if used) and add the tarragon, then set aside over very low heat. Poach the eggs when the pasta is just ready for draining.

Divide the pasta between the plates or bowls. Place a couple of eggs on each portion, then spoon the butter and tarragon over the top. Season with pepper and serve at once with grated Parmesan cheese.

Pasta Carbonara

Serves 4

This is one of the classic Italian dishes.

◆ ¼ cup butter
◆ 1½ cups cooked ham, shredded
◆ 8 eggs
◆ salt and pepper
◆ ⅝ cup light cream
◆ 1 lb. tagliatelle

Method

Melt the butter in a large, heavy-based or non-stick saucepan. Add the ham and cook for 2 minutes. Beat the eggs with seasoning and the cream. Reduce the heat under the pan, if necessary, then pour in the eggs and cook them gently, stirring all the time until they are creamy. Do not cook the eggs until they set and scramble and do not increase the heat to speed up the process or the carbonara will be spoilt.

The pasta should be added to the boiling water at the same time as adding the eggs to the pan. This way, the pasta will be drained and hot, ready to be tipped into the eggs. When the eggs are half set, add the pasta, mix well until the eggs are creamy and serve at once, sprinkled with parsley. Offer Parmesan cheese with the pasta carbonara.

Onion-flavored Hard-cooked Eggs

These hard-cooked eggs are a Lebanese favorite, with a quite distinctive flavor and a beige-brown color when peeled. They are a delicious foil to stews, are occasionally served quartered as meze, and make a fine snack with a salad.

Serves 6

◆ 6 eggs

◆ skins from 6 onions (reserve the onions for another use)

◆ seasoned salt and/or lemon pepper (can be bought prepared in certain stores and delicatessens)

Method

Place the eggs in a saucepan and cover with the onion skins. Pour in enough cold water to cover and turn the heat as low as possible. Simmer very gently for about 6–7 hours, topping up the water when necessary. (Putting a layer of oil over the water will retard evaporation, but it must still be checked occasionally.)

When the time is up, plunge the eggs into cold water and leave to cool before peeling. Serve with the seasoned salt and/or pepper, as desired. The eggs can be kept refrigerated for up to 2 days without losing their flavor.

Cheese-fried Eggs

This dish is simplicity itself and combines two favorite Lebanese fried foods: eggs and cheese. The cheeses most usually used in Lebanon are versions of Kaseri or Haloumi; both are available from Greek, Turkish and Lebanese delicatessens in the West. Italian *pecorino* or a hard goat or ewe cheese would make an authentically strong-tasting substitute.

Serves 4

- *½ tsp. salt*
- *½ tsp. ground cumin*
- *2 tbsp. butter*
- *4 thick slices hard cheese*
- *4 eggs*

Method

In a small salt-cellar or egg cup, mix together the salt and cumin. Reserve.

Heat the butter over medium heat. Add the four cheese slices and fry for about 3 minutes, or until they begin to bubble. Crack an egg over each slice, cover and cook gently, until the egg is just done. Lift the eggy cheeses out with a spatula and serve. Offer the cumin salt; take a pinch and sprinkle over the egg before eating.

Egg and Tomato Favorite

Familiar foods that go together well make this slightly unusual yet reassuring supper dish from Italy.

Serves 4

- *1 lb. tomatoes, peeled and roughly chopped*
- *salt and pepper*
- *4 tbsp. chopped parsley*
- *8 eggs*
- *large knob of butter*
- *1 lb. pasta*
- *freshly grated Parmesan or Cheddar cheese, to serve*

Method

Place the tomatoes in a basin and season them well, then mix in the parsley. Place the eggs in a saucepan, cover with cold water and bring to a boil. Cook for 10 minutes, then drain. Shell the eggs under cold water so as not to burn your fingers and place them in a basin, then cut them into eighths.

Toss the hot eggs and butter into the pasta, then mix in the tomatoes when the butter has melted. Serve at once, topping each portion with grated cheese.

CHAPTER 4

MEAT

. . . .

THERE ARE SOME VERY FAMOUS MEDITERRANEAN

MEAT DISHES – LAMB KLEFTIKO AND MOUSSAKA, FOR

EXAMPLE, ARE A POPULAR CHOICE FOR DINERS IN

GREEK RESTAURANTS WORLDWIDE. HERE YOU WILL

ALSO FIND LESS WELL-KNOWN ONES WHICH ARE

EVERY BIT AS DELICIOUS.

Marinated Roast Veal

Portuguese veal is redder and more full-flavored than we are accustomed to, but this recipe works very well with the veal available to us as the marinade moistens the lean flesh and adds flavor to it.

Serves 6–8

- *about 3½ lb. of lean, boneless veal, such as top of leg or rump*
- *⅞ cup olive oil*
- *4 tbsp. white wine vinegar*
- *1 large red onion, finely chopped*
- *1 garlic clove, chopped*
- *1 red chili, seeded and chopped*
- *2½ tbsp. chopped parsley*
- *salt and pepper*

Method

Put the veal in a non-metallic deep dish that it just fits comfortably. Mix together ⅔ cup of the oil and the remaining ingredients. Pour over the veal, turn the meat, then cover and leave in a cool place for 4 hours, or in the refrigerator for 8, turning occasionally.

Preheat the oven to 450°F. Put the veal on a rack in a roasting pan and brush off any piece of herb, garlic or chili. Reserve the marinade.

Roast the meat for 20 minutes. Pour over 1 tablespoon or so of the remaining oil, lower the oven temperature to 350°F and roast for about 1½ hours, basting a few more times with the cooking juices and remaining oil. Leave to rest for 15 minutes in the oven with the heat turned off and the door propped open.

Bring the remaining marinade to a boil in a small saucepan and simmer for 5 minutes.

Slice the veal and pour the marinade over the slices.

Above : Liver with Mint

Liver with Mint

This Lebanese dish offers an unusual combination of flavors by Western tastes, but is exquisite. If fresh mint is not available, half the quantity of dried mint can be used, although the result will not be as subtle – nor as visually attractive.

Serves 4

- ◆ *4 tbsp. combination of butter and olive oil*
- ◆ *1 onion, finely sliced*
- ◆ *1 garlic clove, crushed*
- ◆ *1 lb. calves' or lambs' liver, very thinly sliced*
- ◆ *flour for dredging*
- ◆ *½ cup red wine vinegar*
- ◆ *2 tbsp. very finely chopped fresh mint*

Method

Heat half the butter and oil over medium-high heat. Sauté the onion until it is limp, add the garlic and continue cooking until the onion is lightly colored. Remove the onion and garlic with a slotted spoon and reserve.

Quickly dredge the liver in the flour and shake off the excess. Add the remaining butter and oil to the pan and sauté the liver slices quickly on both sides. Return the onion and garlic to the pan, pour in the vinegar, and stir in the mint. Cook for about 5 minutes, spooning the sauce over the liver, until the liquid is reduced and glazes the meat.

Beef and Onion Stew

This classic Greek stew can also be made with veal.

Serves 8–10

- ¼ cup butter
- 3 lb. braising steak, cut into 2 in. cubes
- 1¼ cups dry red wine
- 15 oz. can chopped tomatoes
- 4 tbsp. tomato paste
- 1¼ cups boiling water
- 3 tbsp. olive oil
- 3 onions, chopped
- 3 garlic cloves, crushed
- 1 tsp. ground cinnamon
- ½ tsp. dried oregano
- salt and pepper
- 4 tbsp. chopped fresh parsley, to garnish

Method

Melt the butter in a large, heavy saucepan and add the cubed meat. Stir and rearrange the meat to brown evenly on all sides.

Add half of the wine and simmer for 5 minutes. Stir in the chopped tomatoes, tomato paste and boiling water. Cover and simmer for 10 minutes.

Meanwhile, heat the oil in a skillet and cook the onions and garlic for about 5 minutes, or until browned. Transfer to the meat in the saucepan and add the cinnamon, oregano, salt and pepper. Cover the stew and simmer over gentle heat for 1–1½ hours or until the meat is very tender, adding the remaining wine during cooking. Sprinkle with chopped fresh parsley to serve.

Broiled Veal Kabobs

As elsewhere in Portugal, in Madeira often what is sold as veal (*vitela*), is, in fact, young beef from a weaned calf so the meat is much darker than the almost white veal we know. It is also tougher, and on the island a customary way to tenderize it is to marinade it in wine and then cook it threaded on to bay sticks. The *espetada*, as the kabobs are called, are traditionally accompanied with new wine.

Serves 4
- *1¼–1½ lb. veal, cut into 1–1¼ in. cubes*
- *1–2 plump garlic cloves, crushed*
- *1 bay leaf, torn in half*
- *small handful of parsley mixed with a little marjoram, chopped*
- *6 tbsp. medium-bodied red or dry white wine*
- *2 tbsp. olive oil, plus extra for brushing*
- *salt and pepper*

Method
Thread the veal on to four skewers and lay in a single layer in a shallow non-metallic dish.

Mix together the garlic, herbs, wine, oil, and pepper. Pour over the veal, turn the skewers and leave in a cool place for 2 hours, turning occasionally.

Preheat the broiler. Remove the skewers from the marinade and dry on paper towels. Brush lightly with oil and broil, turning occasionally and brushing with oil, until cooked to the degree required.

Sprinkle with salt and serve.

Greek Hamburgers

Greek hamburgers can be served hot or cold, but they should never be overcooked.

Serves 6–8

- 1 lb. ground beef
- 2 slices of bread, crusts removed
- 2 tbsp. milk
- 3 tbsp. olive oil
- ¼ cup butter
- 1 small onion, finely chopped
- 1 garlic clove, crushed
- 1 small carrot, finely grated
- 1 tomato, peeled and chopped
- 4 tbsp. chopped fresh parsley
- 2 tbsp. dry red wine
- salt and pepper
- 1¾ cups all-purpose flour

Method

Place the ground beef in a large mixing bowl. Place the bread on a plate and sprinkle over the milk. Allow to soak for 5 minutes, or until the milk has been absorbed, then add to the ground beef. Mix well to combine. Set aside for the time being.

Heat 1 tablespoon of the olive oil and 1 tablespoon of the butter in a skillet until the butter has melted. Add the onion, garlic, carrot and tomato and sauté for about 7 minutes, or until the onion has browned.

Add the sautéed vegetables to the mixing bowl with the parsley, wine and salt and pepper. Mix thoroughly. Set aside for about 30 minutes.

Sprinkle the flour evenly over a cookie sheet. Using slightly damp hands, shape the meat mixture into burger shapes, then drop into the flour and coat on both sides. Place the coated burgers on a clean cookie sheet, lined with baking parchment.

Heat the remaining olive oil and butter in a large skillet until sizzling. Fry the burgers in batches, cooking for about 5 minutes on each side, taking care when turning them over. Add a little extra olive oil and butter as you cook the batches, if necessary. Transfer the cooked burgers to a warm serving plate while you cook the remaining burgers. Serve warm or cold.

Stewed Steak

A simple and tasty way to serve beef at the meze table. This dish is a specialty of the Greek island of Corfu.

Serves 6–8

- 2¼ lb. stewing steak, cut into ½ in. thick slices
- 4 tbsp. all-purpose flour
- salt and pepper
- 1 tsp. dried thyme
- ¼ cup olive oil
- 6 tbsp. red wine vinegar
- 6 tbsp. water
- 2 garlic cloves, crushed
- 1 tbsp. tomato paste
- 2 tbsp. chopped fresh parsley, to garnish

Method

Place the slices of meat in a mixing bowl and sprinkle over the flour, salt and pepper and the thyme. Toss to coat the meat.

Heat half of the oil in a skillet and cook half of the meat for about 5 minutes, or until evenly browned. Transfer to a plate and repeat with the remaining meat. Return the first batch of meat to the skillet.

Add the vinegar, water, garlic and tomato paste and stir. Bring to a boil, cover, and simmer for 1–1½ hours, or until the meat is tender and the sauce has thickened. Add a little extra water during cooking if necessary. Sprinkle with chopped parsley to serve.

Rich Meat Ragout

This is a good Bolognese-style sauce for ladling over pasta or layering with it.

Serves 4

- 3 tbsp. olive oil
- 1 large onion, chopped
- 2 celery stalks, finely diced
- 2 carrots, finely diced
- 1 green bell pepper, seeded and diced
- 2 garlic cloves, crushed
- 4 oz. rindless smoked bacon, diced
- 2 tsp. dried marjoram
- 1 thyme sprig
- 1 bay leaf
- 1 cup lean ground pork
- 1 cup lean ground braising steak
- salt and pepper
- 1 tbsp. all-purpose flour
- 1 tbsp. tomato paste
- 2 × 14 oz. cans chopped tomatoes
- 1¼ cups dry red wine
- 4 tbsp. chopped parsley
- freshly grated Parmesan cheese, to serve

Method

Heat the oil in a large, heavy-based saucepan. Add the onion, celery, carrots, green bell pepper, garlic, bacon, marjoram, thyme and bay leaf. Cook, stirring, until the onion is slightly softened and the bacon cooked – about 15 minutes.

Add the pork and steak and continue to cook, stirring, for 10 minutes to mix and lightly cook the meats. Stir in plenty of seasoning, the flour and tomato paste. Stir in the tomatoes and wine, then bring the sauce to a boil. Reduce the heat, cover, and simmer the sauce for 1½ hours. Stir the sauce occasionally during cooking.

At the end of cooking, taste and adjust the seasoning before mixing in the parsley and serving the sauce ladled over pasta. Serve with Parmesan cheese.

Steak with Salsa Aside

A really simple steak sauce, this one, with some onion and mushrooms to complement the flavor of the meat. The taste-bud awakener is the salsa aside – a Mexican-style cold sauce of tomato, onion and chili, making this an Italian dish with a difference! Noodles or spaghetti are the ideal pasta for this.

Serves 4

- ◆ 8 oz. ripe tomatoes, peeled
- ◆ 1 red onion, finely chopped
- ◆ 2 fresh green chilis, seeded and chopped
- ◆ 1 garlic clove, crushed
- ◆ salt and pepper
- ◆ 1 tsp. superfine sugar
- ◆ grated zest and juice of ½ lime
- ◆ 3 tbsp. chopped cilantro
- ◆ 1½ lb. lean rump steak, sliced across the grain and cut into strips (see Cook's Tip)
- ◆ 3 tbsp. all-purpose flour
- ◆ large knob of beef dripping or 2 tbsp. oil
- ◆ 1 large onion, halved and thinly sliced
- ◆ 1 bay leaf
- ◆ 2 parsley sprigs
- ◆ 2 thyme sprigs
- ◆ 3 cups mushrooms, sliced
- ◆ 2 cups good beef stock or canned consommé
- ◆ dash of Worcestershire sauce

Method

Make the salsa first but not too far ahead of serving. Halve the tomatoes, discard the cores leading from the stalks, then chop them. Mix with the onion, chilis and garlic. Add plenty of seasoning, the sugar, lime zest and juice, and the cilantro. Mix well. Taste to check the seasoning and set aside.

Toss the steak with the flour and plenty of seasoning. Melt the dripping or heat the oil in a large skillet. When the fat is shimmering hot, add the steak and stir-fry the strips until they are browned. If the fat is hot enough, and particularly if using dripping, the strips will seal, brown and cook quickly. Add the onion and herbs, reduce the heat and cook for 15 minutes, or until the onion is softened slightly. Stir in the mushrooms and cook for a further 15 minutes.

Pour in the stock and add Worcestershire sauce to taste. Bring to a boil, stirring, reduce the heat and simmer gently for 5 minutes. Taste for seasoning and remove the herb sprigs before serving.

> ### COOK'S TIP
>
> When cutting steak for frying as above, slice the meat across the grain, then cut the slices into strips. If the meat is cut with the grain the result is not as tender.

Stewed Meat and Ladies' Fingers

This Lebanese dish is usually made with beef, although lamb may also be used. The ladies' fingers do not have to be parboiled, but if they are not they have a rather glutinous consistency – a trait not despised by the Lebanese, but generally rather disliked in the West. The choice is yours.

Serves 4

- ◆ *2 lb. ladies' fingers*
- ◆ *4 tbsp. combination of butter and olive oil*
- ◆ *2 onions, finely sliced*
- ◆ *1 garlic clove, crushed*
- ◆ *1½ lb. lean braising beef, cut into 1 in. cubes*
- ◆ *3 tbsp. tomato paste*
- ◆ *1½ cups hot beef stock*
- ◆ *salt and pepper*
- ◆ *2 tbsp. red wine vinegar or lemon juice*
- ◆ *2 tbsp. finely chopped cilantro*

Method

Trim the stems off the ladies' fingers. (If you are very careful, and manage to trim the stems without cutting into the inner ribbed section of the top, they will not bleed on cooking, and you can avoid parboiling.)

Bring a large saucepan of water to a boil. Drop in the trimmed ladies' fingers, bring back to a boil, and cook for 3 minutes. Drain thoroughly.

Heat 3 tablespoons of the butter and oil in a heatproof casserole, and sauté the onion over medium heat for 5 minutes, or until limp. Add the garlic and continue to cook for another few minutes, until the onion is lightly colored. Remove the onion with a slotted spoon and add the last 1 tablespoon of butter and oil and the meat. Sauté, turning and stirring, until the meat is browned all over. Add the drained ladies' fingers and fry for about 3 more minutes, then return the onion to the casserole.

Stir the tomato paste into the heated beef stock, season, and pour the liquid over the meat and vegetables. Bring back to a boil, cover and lower the heat. Simmer, stirring occasionally, for about 1 hour 45 minutes, or until the meat is very tender when pierced. Top up the liquid with a little water during cooking, if necessary. Just before serving, stir in the red wine vinegar or lemon juice and the chopped cilantro. Serve immediately.

Pork Steaks Marinated in Olive Oil with Mint, and Broiled

A simple but tasty dish from Portugal. The meat can also be cubed and threaded on skewers with cubes of red bell pepper as illustrated.

Serves 4
- ◆ *4 pork steaks*
- ◆ *salt and pepper*

Marinade
- ◆ *1 onion, chopped*
- ◆ *1 garlic clove, chopped*
- ◆ *leaves from a bunch of mint (about 1–1½ cups)*
- ◆ *2 tbsp. lemon juice*
- ◆ *⅔ cup extra virgin olive oil*

Method

Season the pork with pepper and lay in a shallow non-metallic dish.

To make the marinade, blend the onion, garlic, mint, lemon juice, and oil to a paste and spread over the meat. Cover and leave in a cool place or the refrigerator for 6–8 hours, turning the meat a few times.

Preheat the broiler. Broil the pork for 5–6 minutes on each side, sprinkle with salt and serve with crusty bread and a green salad.

Sausage and Bell Pepper Stew

This is a stovetop version of a Greek dish more traditionally cooked in individual clay bowls and baked in the oven. It's simple fare, likely to be served at home or in the country taverns of Greece.

Serves 6–8
- ◆ 3 tbsp. olive oil
- ◆ 1½ lb. good-quality pork link sausages, pricked all over
- ◆ 2 onions, sliced into rings
- ◆ 5 bell peppers of various colors, seeded and cut into ½ in. strips
- ◆ 1½ lb. tomatoes, peeled and sliced
- ◆ 3 garlic cloves, crushed
- ◆ 2 tsp. dried oregano
- ◆ ½ cup dry red wine
- ◆ salt and pepper
- ◆ chopped fresh sage, to garnish

Method
Heat the oil in a large skillet and add the sausages, turning them as they cook, until they are evenly browned on all sides. Place the browned sausages on paper towels to drain.

Add the onion to the skillet with the bell peppers and cook for about 10 minutes, or until softened. Stir in the tomatoes, garlic and oregano.

Return the sausages to the pan and add the wine. Season with salt and pepper and simmer, covered, for about 1 hour, or until the sausages are cooked through, adding a little extra water if necessary. Serve sprinkled with chopped fresh sage.

Meat and Rice Balls in Lemon Sauce

This Greek dish is a cross between a hearty soup and stew.

Serves 8–10

- ◆ *1 lb. ground pork*
- ◆ *¾ cup long-grain rice*
- ◆ *1 large onion, finely chopped*
- ◆ *2 garlic cloves, crushed*
- ◆ *4 tbsp. very finely chopped fresh parsley*
- ◆ *2 tbsp. chopped fresh mint*
- ◆ *1 tsp. dried oregano*
- ◆ *1 egg yolk*
- ◆ *salt and pepper*
- ◆ *flour for dredging*
- ◆ *3 tbsp. olive oil*
- ◆ *3 eggs, beaten*
- ◆ *juice of 2 lemons, strained*
- ◆ *chopped fresh parsley, to garnish*

Method

Combine the ground pork, rice, onion, garlic and herbs in a large mixing bowl. Add the egg yolk and season with salt and pepper.

Mix thoroughly to combine all the ingredients. Using slightly damp hands, shape the mixture into 2-inch balls and dredge with flour.

Place the olive oil in a large, deep skillet with the meat balls. Add enough boiling water to just cover the meat balls. Cover and simmer for 35–40 minutes, or until the meat and rice are cooked, adding a little extra water to keep the meat balls covered during cooking if necessary.

To make the lemon sauce, beat together the eggs and lemon juice until frothy. Beat in 2 tablespoons of the cooking liquid from the meat balls, beating vigorously to prevent curdling. Remove the skillet from the heat and pour the egg mixture over the meat balls. Return the skillet to the heat and stir continuously, until thickened. Do not allow the sauce to boil. Transfer the meat balls and sauce to a warm serving dish and garnish with chopped fresh parsley.

Pork and Pasta Rolls

This Italian dish takes quite a bit of preparation, but it does taste delicious!

Serves 4

- *1 lb. ground pork*
- *½ cup fresh white bread crumbs*
- *1 onion, finely chopped*
- *1 tbsp. chopped rosemary*
- *2 tbsp. chopped parsley*
- *2 eggs, beaten*
- *salt and pepper*
- *½ quantity carrot-flavored pasta dough (see p.13)*
- *1¼ cups dry cider*
- *2½ cups chicken stock*
- *3 tbsp. butter*
- *2 tbsp. all-purpose flour*
- *rosemary sprigs to garnish (optional)*

Method

Mix the pork, bread crumbs, onion, rosemary, parsley and half the beaten egg. Add plenty of seasoning and pound the mixture until all the ingredients are thoroughly combined.

Roll out the dough into an oblong measuring slightly larger than 17 x 10 inches. Trim the edges, then brush the pasta with beaten egg. Spread the meat mixture all over the roll, leaving a narrow border around the edge. Roll up the pasta from the long end. Seal the end of the roll with more beaten egg and press it down on the roll with a blunt knife.

Preheat the oven to 350°F. Prepare a large saucepan of boiling water. Cut the roll in half or quarters, depending on the size of the saucepan. Carefully lower the pieces of roll into the water and simmer for 3 minutes. Wrapping a couple of bands of folded foil around the roll helps with lowering it into the water and lifting it out again; otherwise use a large fish slice and slotted spoon to drain the pieces of roll. Cut the roll into 16 slices and place them in an ovenproof casserole.

Heat the cider and stock together, then pour them over the rolls, cover and bake for 1 hour. Meanwhile, beat the butter into the flour. Transfer the cooked rolls to a serving dish or individual plates and keep hot. Bring the cooking juices to a boil in a saucepan, then gradually whisk in the butter and flour paste. Boil for 3 minutes, then taste for seasoning. Spoon a little of the sauce over the rolls and offer the rest separately. Garnish with fresh rosemary sprigs if you like.

Pork with Dates and Ginger

Serve this sweet and slightly spicy Italian dish with plain fine noodles or tagliatelle and a fresh onion salad (see Cook's Tip).

Serves 4

- ◆ 2 tbsp. oil
- ◆ 2 oz. fresh ginger root, peeled and chopped
- ◆ 1 cinnamon stick
- ◆ 1½ lb. lean boneless pork, diced
- ◆ salt and pepper
- ◆ 4 oz. fresh dates
- ◆ ⅝ cup fresh orange juice
- ◆ ⅝ cup water
- ◆ ⅝ cup sour cream

Method

Heat the oil in a skillet. Add the ginger, cinnamon and pork. Sprinkle in plenty of seasoning, then cook, until the pork is lightly browned and cooked through.

Meanwhile, slit the dates and remove their stones, then rub off their papery skins and slice the fruit. Add the orange juice and water to the pork. Bring to a boil, reduce the heat and simmer hard for 10 minutes. Stir in the dates, simmer for 5 minutes and taste for seasoning.

Remove the pan from the heat, swirl in the sour cream and serve at once, ladled over individual portions of pasta.

COOK'S TIP

Fresh onion salad: Thinly slice 2 red or white onions. Separate the slices into rings and place them in a bowl of iced water. Leave to soak for 30 minutes, or up to an hour. Drain well and pat dry on paper towels. Trim and roughly chop 1 bunch of watercress. Cut the tops from a tub of cress. Mix both types of cress and the onions. Sprinkle with salt, a little lemon juice and a little olive oil. Dust with paprika and serve.

Right : Pork with Dates and Ginger

Lentil and Pork Stew

This is a typical, robust and filling country dish from Portugal.

Serves 6

- *1 lb. green or brown lentils*
- *2 onions, chopped*
- *1 carrot, chopped*
- *4 garlic cloves, halved lengthwise*
- *1 red bell pepper, cored, seeded, and chopped*
- *8 oz. black pudding*
- *8 oz. chouriço*
- *8 oz. fresh picnic shoulder, cut into chunks*
- *1 bay leaf, torn almost in half*
- *several sprigs of parsley*
- *½ tsp. paprika*
- *2 tbsp. olive oil*
- *salt and pepper*

Method

Put all the ingredients into a heavy-based flameproof casserole. Add sufficient water to cover by about 1 inch, bring to a boil and then simmer gently for 30–40 minutes until the meats and lentils are tender and there is very little surplus liquid. Top up with boiling water as necessary.

Slice the black pudding and chouriço, and return to the stew. Stir together and serve.

Rabbit in Red Wine

The authentic wine to use in this Portuguese recipe is a red Dão, the best-known Portuguese red table wine. It is smooth, fruity, and full-bodied, so makes this a robust rabbit dish. There is no problem about the choice of wine to serve with the dish – the same that has been used in the cooking!

Serves 4

- ◆ *1 rabbit, jointed*
- ◆ *2 onions, chopped*
- ◆ *3 garlic cloves, crushed*
- ◆ *5 oz. presunto or bacon, chopped*
- ◆ *2 tbsp. olive oil*
- ◆ *1 tsp. all-purpose flour*
- ◆ *1 cup light game, chicken, or veal stock*
- ◆ *1 cup red wine*
- ◆ *bouquet garni*
- ◆ *salt and pepper*
- ◆ *chopped parsley, to garnish*

Method
Cook the rabbit portions, onions, garlic, and presunto or bacon in the olive oil in a heavy flameproof casserole, until the rabbit portions are brown and the onions softened. Remove the rabbit portions.

Sprinkle the flour over the onion mixture and stir it in for 1–2 minutes. Pour in the stock slowly, stirring constantly, then add the wine and bring to a boil. Simmer for 2–3 minutes before returning the rabbit portions to the casserole with the bouquet garni and seasoning. Cover tightly and cook gently until the rabbit is tender.

Discard the bouquet garni, sprinkle with chopped parsley and serve.

Right : Lamb Kabobs

Lamb Kabobs

Variations of ground "rolls" are found all over the Middle East, Greece, Turkey and the Balkan states, and are well-known in the West from their frequent appearance on kabob house menus. What distinguishes the national versions are the spicing and special ingredients and the method of cooking. This Lebanese recipe is satisfying but simple.

Serves 6–8

- ◆ *4 slices of bread, crusts removed and cubed (about 3 cups)*
- ◆ *1 garlic clove, crushed*
- ◆ *2 lb. ground lamb*
- ◆ *2 small onions, grated*
- ◆ *¼ cup ground cumin*
- ◆ *½ tsp. cayenne pepper*
- ◆ *3 tbsp. finely chopped parsley*
- ◆ *1 egg*
- ◆ *salt and pepper*
- ◆ *lemon wedges*

Method
Place the bread in a small bowl and add enough water to dampen them – about 4–5 tablespoons. Add the garlic and, with your hands, mash the bread and garlic with the water. Leave to stand for 10 minutes.

In a large bowl, mix together the ground lamb, grated onion, cumin, cayenne and parsley. Work with your hands to combine. Knead in the bread paste, the egg and seasoning to taste, until everything is mixed and the meat has absorbed the liquid.

With your hands, roll the meat into 6–8 long cylinders. Pass a skewer through each cylinder and pat the meat to secure it.

Cook the kabobs over gray-ashed coals for about 20 minutes, until they are brown on all sides. Serve with lemon wedges.

Lisbon Liver

Thinly sliced liver which is marinated, then cooked with presunto, is traditionally associated with Lisbon, but is popular throughout Portugal.

Serves 4

◆ *1 lb. lamb's liver, thinly sliced*
◆ *4 garlic cloves, crushed*
◆ *1 bay leaf*
◆ *salt and pepper*
◆ *¾ cup dry white wine*
◆ *1 tbsp. white wine vinegar*
◆ *3 tbsp. shortening or olive oil*
◆ *2 oz. presunto, prosciutto, or bacon, chopped*

Method

Put the liver into a dish, add the garlic, bay leaf, and seasoning, and pour over the wine and vinegar. Cover and leave in a cool place for at least 4 hours, preferably overnight.

Remove the liver from the wine and pat dry with paper towels. Reserve the wine, discarding the bay leaf.

Heat the shortening or oil, add the ham or bacon and cook until crisp. Add the liver and cook for about 3 minutes on each side. Transfer the liver and ham or bacon to a warmed plate, cover and keep warm.

Stir the wine into the pan and boil rapidly until reduced by about half. Pour over the liver.

Spicy Lamb Stew with Mint and Sage

This is a traditional Greek pilaf for which lamb or veal can be used.

Serves 6–8

- ¼ cup olive oil
- 2 lb. lean lamb tenderloin, cut into 1-in. cubes
- 1 onion, chopped
- 2 carrots, diced
- ½ cup dry white wine
- salt and pepper
- ⅔ cup flaked almonds
- 3¾ cups water
- 1⅓ cups long-grain rice
- ⅓ cup golden raisins
- ⅓ cup raisins
- ½ tsp. dried sage
- 1 tsp. dried mint

Method

Heat the oil in a large saucepan. Add the cubed meat and cook, turning frequently, until evenly browned. Add the onion and carrots and cook for about 5 minutes. Stir in the wine and season with salt and pepper. Bring to a boil, then cover and cook for 10 minutes.

Meanwhile, toast the almonds, either under the broiler or in a heavy-based skillet, until they are golden. Set aside.

Stir the water into the meat mixture and continue to simmer for a further 30 minutes, stirring occasionally. Add the rice, golden raisins, raisins, sage and mint to the stew and adjust the seasoning, if necessary. Simmer, covered, for a further 30–35 minutes, or until the rice is cooked and the meat is tender, adding a little extra water during cooking if necessary. Scatter the toasted flaked almonds over the stew and serve hot.

Lamb Kleftiko

Authentic Greek *kleftiko* is cooked to the point where the meat just falls off the bone. The secret is long, slow cooking in a foil package to allow the flavors to stay trapped inside until the meat is so tender that it literally melts in the mouth. A large wedge of lemon is served with the meat to help cleanse the palate.

Serves 8
- 8 lamb chops
- 4 garlic cloves, cut into slivers
- ¼ cup butter, melted
- 3 tbsp. lemon juice
- salt and pepper
- 1 tbsp. dried oregano
- 1 tbsp. dried mint

Method
Preheat the oven to 350°F. Using a small, sharp knife, make incisions in the chops and insert the slivers of garlic into them. Place each chop in the center of a 12-in. square piece of aluminum foil.

Distribute the remaining ingredients between the chops and gather up the foil, pinching it together at the top to completely encase and seal in the chops.

Arrange the foil packages on a cookie sheet and cook for 1½–2 hours, or until the meat is cooked through and very tender. Serve the packages closed to be opened by each diner.

Lamb and Pasta Hotpot

This is a heart-warming winter stew from Italy. Beef, pork or bacon may all be used instead of lamb. Offer some crusty bread to mop up the juices.

Serves 4
- ◆ 1 tbsp. oil
- ◆ 1¼ lb. lean boneless lamb, cubed
- ◆ 1 onion, chopped
- ◆ 2 carrots, diced
- ◆ 2 rosemary sprigs
- ◆ salt and pepper
- ◆ 2½ cups beer
- ◆ 2½ cups water
- ◆ 8 oz. frozen peas
- ◆ 1 lb. pasta spirals
- ◆ ⅝ cup sour cream
- ◆ paprika
- ◆ croûtons, to serve

Method

Heat the oil in a large flameproof casserole or heavy-based saucepan. Add the lamb and brown the cubes all over. Stir in the onion, carrots, rosemary sprigs and seasoning. Cook, stirring, for a few minutes, then add the beer and water. Bring just to a boil, reduce the heat and cover the pan. Leave the hotpot to simmer for 1¼ hours, stirring occasionally until the lamb is tender and the cooking liquor is well flavored.

Taste for seasoning, then add the peas. Bring back to a boil, reduce the heat and cover the pot. Simmer for 15 minutes. Add the pasta, stir well, then bring back to a boil. Partially cover the pan and cook for 5 minutes, allowing the hotpot to only just boil.

Top individual portions of the hotpot with sour cream and sprinkle with paprika. Sprinkle with croûtons and serve piping hot.

Lamb Knuckle Stew

Lamb knuckle is an economical dish in any guise; in Lebanon it is often stewed with green beans, or as here, with garbanzo beans.

Serves 4
- *1 tbsp. olive oil*
- *2 onions, sliced*
- *3 garlic cloves, finely chopped*
- *1 tsp. allspice*
- *2 tsp. ground cumin*
- *pinch of crushed dried red pepper flakes*
- *1 bay leaf, crushed*
- *4 meaty knuckles of lamb (about 12 oz. each)*
- *2 × 14 oz. cans garbanzo beans, drained and rinsed*
- *2 × 14 oz. cans chopped tomatoes*
- *2 cups lamb or beef stock*
- *salt and pepper*
- *1 lemon*
- *1 cup chopped cilantro*

Method
Preheat the oven to 475°F. Pour the oil into a casserole in which the knuckles will fit in one layer with space to spare. Heat over medium heat, add the sliced onion and sauté for 4 minutes, then add the garlic and continue cooking until the onion and garlic are limp and lightly colored, about 6 minutes.

Remove the hot onions with a slotted spoon to a large bowl, stir in the spices and bay leaf, and reserve. Add the knuckles to the casserole, turning in the oil to brown them. Transfer the casseroled lamb to the oven, and bake for 35 minutes, turning the knuckles occasionally.

Add the garbanzo beans, tomatoes and stock to the onions in the bowl and mix together. Remove the casserole from the oven, pour the garbanzo bean and tomato mixture over the knuckles and season to taste. Bring the stew to a boil on top of the stove, then cover and continue baking for another hour on the lower shelf of the oven. Test the knuckle with a knife for doneness; it should pierce easily.

Squeeze over the juice from the lemon and sprinkle the cilantro over the stew. Serve immediately.

Moussaka

Recognized as the national dish of Greece – sliced eggplants layered with onions and ground lamb, then topped with béchamel sauce.

Serves 10–12

- ◆ 5 large eggplants, trimmed and sliced lengthwise
- ◆ salt
- ◆ olive oil for brushing
- ◆ 2 cups fresh white bread crumbs
- ◆ 6 oz. Feta cheese, grated
- ◆ 5½ cups béchamel sauce (see p.11)

Meat sauce

- ◆ 2 tbsp. olive oil
- ◆ 4 onions, roughly chopped
- ◆ 2½ lb. lean ground lamb
- ◆ 2 × 15 oz. cans chopped tomatoes
- ◆ 3 garlic cloves, crushed
- ◆ ½ tsp. ground cinnamon
- ◆ pinch of ground allspice
- ◆ salt and pepper
- ◆ 4 tbsp. tomato paste
- ◆ ½ cup dry red wine

Method

Lay the slices of eggplants out on the work surface and sprinkle evenly with salt on both sides. Allow to "sweat" for 30 minutes, then rinse the slices thoroughly under cold running water.

Lay as many slices of eggplant as possible on the rack of a broiler pan and brush generously with olive oil. Broil for 5–10 minutes, turning the slices over and brushing again with olive oil, until they are golden-brown on both sides. Set aside and repeat with the remaining slices of eggplant.

Grease an 11 × 15 × 3-inch baking dish with olive oil and sprinkle evenly with the bread crumbs.

To make the meat sauce, heat the olive oil in a large, heavy saucepan and sauté the onion until softened. Add the ground lamb and stir. Cook, stirring frequently, for about 10 minutes, or until the meat is no longer pink. Add the tomatoes, garlic and spices and season with salt and pepper. Stir in the tomato paste and the red wine.

Reduce the heat, cover, and simmer the sauce for about 45 minutes, adding a little water if necessary. Remove the cover for the last 15 minutes of the cooking time to allow all of the moisture to evaporate. Set the sauce aside to cool slightly.

Preheat the oven to 350°F. Arrange a layer of sliced eggplant in the bottom of the prepared dish and cover with a layer of the meat sauce. Add another layer of the eggplant slices and another of the meat sauce. Continue layering in this fashion, finishing with a layer of sliced eggplant. Carefully pour the béchamel sauce on top of the dish and spread evenly. Sprinkle with the grated Feta cheese and bake in the oven for about 1 hour, or until the top is golden-brown and the moussaka is heated through. Serve warm.

Meatballs in Tomato Sauce

This rich, tasty Greek dish can be made well in advance and kept in the refrigerator – in fact, it tastes better reheated the next day.

Serves 6–8
- 1½ lb. ground lamb
- 2 slices wholewheat bread
- ¼ cup milk
- 1 tbsp. olive oil
- 1 onion, chopped
- 1 tomato, peeled, seeded and chopped
- ⅔ cup long-grain rice
- 1 tbsp. chopped fresh mint
- pinch of ground cinnamon
- 2 tbsp. chopped fresh parsley
- 1 egg, beaten
- ¼ cup red wine
- salt and pepper
- 5 cups water
- 4 tbsp. tomato paste
- 1 garlic clove, crushed
- chopped fresh parsley, to garnish

Method
Place the ground lamb in a large mixing bowl. Remove the crusts from the bread and place the bread on a plate. Sprinkle over the milk and allow to soak for 10 minutes, or until all the milk has been soaked up into the bread. Add the bread to the mixing bowl. Using your hand, mix the meat and bread together thoroughly.

Heat the olive oil in a small saucepan and sauté the onion and chopped tomato flesh for about 5 minutes. Add to the mixing bowl with the rice, mint, cinnamon, parsley, beaten egg, wine and salt and pepper. Mix well to combine all the ingredients.

Place the water in a large, deep skillet and stir in the tomato paste. Add the garlic and heat gently to bring to a boil. Simmer for 5 minutes.

Using slightly damp hands, shape the meat mixture into round balls, each about the size of a golf ball, and carefully place them in the simmering tomato sauce. Cover the skillet and cook for about 30 minutes, or until the rice is cooked and the sauce has thickened. Serve garnished with chopped parsley.

Right : Meatballs in Tomato Sauce

Chunks of Lamb in Phyllo Pastry

This Greek dish would be perfect for a meze picnic. Easily made in advance, it can also be frozen unbaked, then thawed and finished off in the oven when required.

Serves 10–15
- ◆ 8 lb. leg of lamb
- ◆ 4 garlic cloves, cut into slivers
- ◆ salt and pepper
- ◆ 2 tsp. dried oregano
- ◆ 1½ cups butter, melted
- ◆ 3 tbsp. lemon juice
- ◆ 2 carrots, peeled
- ◆ 2 celery stalks, trimmed
- ◆ 1 onion, quartered
- ◆ 1 lb. phyllo pastry dough, thawed if frozen
- ◆ 8 cups fresh white bread crumbs
- ◆ 8 oz. Feta cheese, grated

Method

Preheat the oven to 375°F. Using a sharp knife, make small incisions all over the lamb and insert the slivers of garlic into them. Place the lamb in a roasting pan. Season with salt and pepper and sprinkle over the oregano. Drizzle over a little of the melted butter and pour over the lemon juice. Add the carrot, celery and onion to the pan and roast the lamb for 2–2½ hours, until the meat is tender and the juices run clear. Transfer the meat to a chopping board and cut the meat into 1-inch chunks, discarding the fat and bone. Allow the chunks of meat to cool.

Take one sheet of the phyllo pastry dough, keeping the remainder covered with a slightly damp cloth, and brush lightly with melted butter. Fold the sheet in half. Brush once again with melted butter, then sprinkle over a few of the bread crumbs.

Place a few chunks of meat toward one end of the phyllo and sprinkle over a little of the cheese. Fold up around the filling, enclosing it securely, and place seamside down on a lightly oiled cookie sheet. Repeat with the remaining phyllo pastry dough and filling. Brush the packages with the remaining melted butter and bake for about 30 minutes, or until the pastry has turned crisp and golden.

CHAPTER 5

VEGETABLES, GRAINS AND SALADS

· · · ·

Salads are popular in this hot climate, and here the locally produced olive oils and the sun-ripened tomatoes bursting with flavor can really come into their own. Bell peppers and eggplants are favorite vegetables, making an appearance in many dishes, and pulses — staple food in impoverished communities — are frequently used to provide filling and nutritious meals.

Zucchini with Walnuts

Serves 4–6

- ◆ *5 tbsp. butter or olive oil*
- ◆ *1½ lb. zucchini, washed, trimmed and thinly sliced*
- ◆ *salt and pepper*
- ◆ *scant 1 cup walnut halves, chopped*
- ◆ *large pinch of allspice*
- ◆ *2 tbsp. finely chopped parsley*

Method

Heat the butter or oil in a heavy skillet and sauté the zucchini, stirring them for about 5 minutes, or until soft. Season with salt and pepper, then stir in the walnuts and allspice. Combine well, take off the heat and scatter the parsley on top. Serve immediately.

Cauliflower Baked with Tomatoes and Feta

This dish is enlivened with a strong flavor of tomatoes combined with the typically Greek use of ground cinnamon to give that extra-special taste.

Serves 4–6

- *6 tbsp. olive oil*
- *1 onion, sliced*
- *2 garlic cloves, crushed*
- *8 tomatoes, peeled and chopped*
- *large pinch of ground cinnamon*
- *2 tsp. dried oregano*
- *salt and pepper*
- *1 large cauliflower, cut into flowerets*
- *1 tbsp. lemon juice*
- *¾ cup Feta cheese, grated*

Method

Heat 2–3 tablespoons of olive oil in a heavy-based skillet and sauté the onion and garlic for 3–4 minutes, or until the onion has softened.

Add the chopped tomatoes, cinnamon and oregano and season with salt and pepper. Stir and simmer, covered, for 5 minutes.

Preheat the oven to 375°F. Add the cauliflower to the tomato mixture, cover, and simmer for a further 10–15 minutes or until the cauliflower is just tender. Remove from the heat.

Transfer the cauliflower and tomato mixture to a large, shallow dish and drizzle over the remaining olive oil. Sprinkle over the lemon juice and grated Feta. Bake for 45–50 minutes, or until the cauliflower is soft and the cheese has melted. Serve warm.

Garbanzo Bean Stew

Garbanzo beans are eaten so frequently in Portugal they are sold from, and indeed by, the sackful in open markets. Being cheap, nutraitious and filling, they are often added to casseroles and stews to "stretch" the meat content.

Serves 4–6

- *1 cup garbanzo beans, soaked overnight and drained*
- *2 tbsp. olive oil*
- *4 oz. piece of presunto or smoked bacon, cut into strips*
- *1 lb. pork shoulder, cubed*
- *5 oz. chouriço, thickly sliced*
- *1 large onion, chopped*
- *2 plump garlic cloves, chopped*
- *1 carrot, chopped*
- *1 celery stalk, chopped*
- *1 leek, chopped*
- *1 bouquet garni*
- *1 cup vegetable, veal, or brown veal stock*
- *salt and pepper*
- *handful of chopped parsley*

Method

Put the garbanzo beans into a saucepan and just cover with water. Bring to a boil, then cover and simmer while preparing the remaining ingredients.

Heat the oil in another saucepan, add the presunto or bacon, and pork and chouriço, and brown evenly. Remove using a slotted spoon. Stir the onion, garlic, carrot, celery, and leek into the pan and fry until softened and lightly browned.

Stir some of the water from the garbanzo beans into the onion mixture to dislodge the sediment on the bottom of the pan. Then add the remaining water and the beans. Return the meats to the pan and add the bouquet garni and stock. Simmer gently, partly covered, for about 1¼ hours. There should only be a little water left in the pan at the end of cooking; if necessary, leave the pan uncovered so that the excess water will evaporate, or add more water if the pan becomes dry. Discard the bouquet garni, season and stir in the parsley before serving.

Right : Garbanzo Bean Stew

Artichoke Heart and Fava Bean Stew

This classic Greek dish requires a little patience in preparing the vegetables and the sauce, but the end result is very much worth the effort.

Serves 6–8

- *juice of 3 lemons*
- *2½ cups water*
- *8 fresh globe artichokes*
- *3 tbsp. olive oil*
- *1 large onion, finely chopped*
- *3 garlic cloves, crushed*
- *2 lb. fresh fava beans, podded, washed and drained (or 1 lb. frozen fava beans)*
- *⅔ cup thinly sliced fennel*
- *salt and pepper*
- *½ tsp. sugar*

Sauce

- *¼ cup olive oil*
- *1 tbsp. all-purpose flour*
- *juice of 1 lemon*
- *salt and pepper*

Method

Place the juice of 2 of the lemons in a large bowl with the water. To prepare the artichokes, using a pair of kitchen scissors, cut off all but 1 inch of the stems and cut away the tough outer leaves. Cut off about 2½ inches from the top of each artichoke. Open out the leaves of the artichokes and, using a teaspoon, scrape out the hairy chokes and discard. Submerge the prepared artichokes in the lemon water.

Heat the olive oil in a large, deep skillet and sauté the onion and garlic for 3–4 minutes, until the onion has softened. Add the fava beans to the pan and cook for a further 3–4 minutes. Add the artichokes, fennel, salt and pepper, sugar and the remaining lemon juice. Add enough water to the pan to almost cover, then reduce the heat, place the lid on the pan and simmer for 50–60 minutes, or until the vegetables are tender, adding a little extra during cooking if necessary.

Using a slotted spoon, transfer the artichokes and beans to a warm serving plate and tent with foil to keep warm. To make the sauce, heat 3 tablespoons of olive oil in a medium-sized saucepan and stir in the flour to make a thick paste. Cook the paste for about 1–2 minutes, or until it turns a light golden color.

Beat the lemon juice and then the cooking juices from the vegetables into the saucepan. Cook over gentle heat, stirring continuously, until the sauce has thickened and there are no lumps. Season with salt and pepper. Remove the foil tent from the vegetables and pour the sauce over them. Serve warm with plenty of bread to mop up.

Garbanzo Beans with Spinach

To maintain the low heat that is necessary for this Portuguese dish, it is best to use a heat-diffusing mat.

Serves 4
- ◆ 8 oz. garbanzo beans, soaked overnight and drained
- ◆ 2¼ lb. spinach
- ◆ 1 large onion, thinly sliced
- ◆ 4 garlic cloves, chopped
- ◆ salt and pepper
- ◆ paprika
- ◆ ½ cup beef stock
- ◆ 4 tbsp. olive oil

Method
Cook the garbanzo beans in simmering water for about 1 hour. Drain thoroughly.

Put one-third of the spinach in a heavy flameproof casserole; cover with half the onion and garlic, then half the garbanzo beans, seasoning each layer with salt, pepper, and paprika.

Repeat the layers, ending with the remaining spinach. Pour over the stock and then pour the oil evenly over the top. Cover tightly and cook gently until the garbanzo beans are tender and there is no surplus liquid; if necessary, add more stock, or water, to prevent the mixture drying out.

Spinach Croquettes

In this Greek recipe, rye crispbread crumbs are used to coat the croquettes before frying. If rye crispbread is not available, whole wheat flour is a good substitute.

Serves 6–8
- ◆ 2 tbsp. butter
- ◆ 1 onion, very finely chopped
- ◆ 2 lb. fresh spinach, roughly chopped
- ◆ 6 oz. Feta cheese, grated
- ◆ 3 eggs, 2 separated
- ◆ salt and pepper
- ◆ 1½ cups fresh white bread crumbs
- ◆ 1½ cups rye crispbread crumbs
- ◆ olive oil for shallow frying

Method
Melt the butter in a skillet and add the onion. Sauté for about 3 minutes to soften, then add the spinach. Cook for a further 5 minutes, or until the spinach is softened, then remove from the heat.

Transfer the spinach mixture to a medium-sized mixing bowl and stir in the cheese, whole egg and the egg yolks. Season with salt and pepper and stir in the fresh bread crumbs.

Place the crispbread crumbs on one plate and the egg whites on another. Using slightly damp hands, shape the mixture into small croquettes. Roll the croquettes in the crispbread to coat, then in the egg white, and finally in the crispbread again.

Heat the oil in a skillet and shallow fry the croquettes in batches for about 5–8 minutes, or until golden-brown and cooked through, turning and rearranging them frequently during cooking. Using a slotted spoon, transfer the croquettes to a dish lined with paper towels to drain. Serve warm or cold.

Fettuccine with Garlicky Creamed Spinach

This tasty Italian recipe is quick and easy to prepare. Serve immediately with plenty of freshly grated Parmesan cheese.

Serves 4–6

- ◆ 1 lb. dried fettuccine
- ◆ dash of olive oil
- ◆ 2 tbsp. butter
- ◆ 3 garlic cloves, crushed
- ◆ 1 lb. frozen chopped spinach, thawed and well drained
- ◆ 1¼ cups light cream
- ◆ pinch of freshly grated mace
- ◆ salt and pepper
- ◆ ⅔ cup freshly grated Parmesan cheese, plus extra to serve

Method

Bring a large saucepan of water to a boil, and add the fettuccine with a dash of olive oil. Cook for about 8 minutes, stirring occasionally, until tender. Drain and set aside, covered, to keep warm.

Melt the butter in a large skillet and sauté the garlic for 1–2 minutes, then add the spinach. Cook over medium heat for about 5 minutes, stirring frequently, until the moisture has evaporated.

Add the cream and mace and season with salt and pepper. Toss in the fettuccine and Parmesan cheese, stir, and cook for a final minute. Serve with extra freshly grated Parmesan cheese.

Fried Potatoes

These fried potatoes are one of the spiciest dishes from the Lebanese kitchen, where cooks otherwise treat fresh chilis with respect. They are unashamedly oily and garlicky as well, so they are not for the faint-hearted or dyspeptic!

Serves 4–6
- ½ cup olive oil
- 1½ lb. potatoes, peeled and chopped into small pieces
- salt and pepper
- 3 garlic cloves, crushed
- 2 hot chilis, seeded and chopped
- 1 cup finely chopped cilantro

Method
Heat the olive oil and drop in the potatoes. Fry over medium-hot heat and season to taste. Continue cooking for about 20 minutes until the potatoes are soft. Add the garlic and chilis, and gently toss the potatoes over the heat. Sprinkle over the cilantro and serve.

Right : Garlic Roasted Potatoes

Garlic Roasted Potatoes

These Greek-style potatoes taste as good as they sound. Cooked with fresh lemon juice and oregano – once tasted, you'll realize there's no other way to roast potatoes.

Serves 6–8
- 2 lb. large potatoes, peeled
- ¼ cup olive oil
- ½ cup lemon juice
- 2 tsp. dried oregano
- 3 garlic cloves, very finely chopped
- salt and pepper
- ½ cup water

Method
Preheat the oven to 450°F. Cut the potatoes into quarters or eighths lengthwise and place in a large, shallow baking dish.

Add the remaining ingredients and stir the potatoes to coat. Bake at the top of the oven, uncovered, for 1 hour, or until lightly golden, crisp on the outside and soft inside. Rearrange the potatoes, and add a little more water during cooking, if necessary.

Stuffed Tomatoes

These Portuguese-style tomatoes are very versatile – they go well with roast or broiled meat or poultry, or fish; they can also be served as part of an all-vegetable meal, or as an appetizer.

Serves 4
- *4 very large, ripe, well-flavored tomatoes, or 8 smaller ones, halved horizontally*
- *2 handfuls fresh bread crumbs*
- *2 garlic cloves, finely chopped*
- *handful of chopped parsley*
- *3 tbsp. olive oil*
- *2 eggs, beaten*
- *salt and pepper*

Method
Preheat the oven to 400°F. Scoop out the insides of the tomatoes carefully. Season the inside of the tomatoes, turn them upside down and leave to drain.

Mix together the remaining ingredients. Place the tomatoes the right way up in a greased baking dish and fill with the bread crumb mixture.

Bake in the oven for about 15 minutes. Serve hot.

Meatless Stuffed Vegetables

This recipe originates from the island of Crete, where the use of rice as the main ingredient for stuffings is common. The addition of raisins and pine nuts makes this a truly Cretan creation.

Serves 8–10

- 8–10 firm, ripe vegetables, including tomatoes, bell peppers, zucchini and eggplants
- 6 tbsp. olive oil
- 6 scallions, finely chopped
- 1⅓ cups long-grain rice
- 2 garlic cloves, crushed
- 1 tsp. ground cinnamon
- ½ cup seedless raisins
- ½ cup toasted pine nuts
- salt and pepper
- 4 tbsp. chopped fresh parsley
- 3 tbsp. chopped fresh mint

Method

To prepare the vegetables, slice the tops off the tomatoes, bell peppers, zucchini and eggplants. Scoop out the seeds and flesh from the tomatoes and place in a bowl. Do the same with the eggplants and zucchini, remembering to discard the bitter seeds from the eggplants. Scoop out the seeds from the bell peppers and discard. Keep each vegetable top intact because they provide the lids for the vegetables when they are stuffed.

In a large skillet, heat 2 tablespoons of the olive oil and add the scallions. Cook for 3 minutes, then stir in the rice, garlic, cinnamon, raisins, pine nuts and the seeds and pulp reserved from the vegetables. Add enough water to cover the rice and simmer, covered, for 7–10 minutes, or until the rice is tender and the majority of the liquid has been absorbed.

Stir the seasoning and herbs into the rice filling and remove from the heat. Preheat the oven to 350°F. Stuff the vegetables with the rice filling and place the tops on each vegetable. Arrange the vegetables in a large roasting pan and pour in enough water to just cover the base of the pan.

Drizzle over the remaining olive oil and bake for 50–60 minutes, or until the vegetables are tender. Baste the stuffed vegetables several times during cooking, but try not to rearrange them as they may break apart. These can be served warm, but are just as delicious served cold.

Potatoes with Bacon and Onion

This interesting potato dish from Portugal can be served with simply cooked chicken, with regular omelets or scrambled eggs, or can be topped with poached eggs.

Serves 4–6
- *2¼ lb. potatoes*
- *1 onion, chopped*
- *3 tbsp. olive oil*
- *4–6 oz. piece smoked bacon, chopped*
- *¾ cup chopped cilantro or parsley*
- *salt and pepper*

Method

Boil the potatoes until tender. Drain thoroughly and slice.

Meanwhile, fry the onion in the oil until softened but not colored. Remove and keep warm.

Add the bacon to the pan and cook until brown and crisp. Add the potatoes and cook until browned on both sides.

Stir the onion, cilantro or parsley, and seasoning into the potatoes gently. Warm through and serve.

Rigatoni with Bell Peppers and Garlic

The raw garlic added at the end of the recipe gives this dish the true taste of the Mediterranean.

Serves 4
- ¾ lb. dried rigatoni (large tubes)
- dash of olive oil, plus 4 tbsp.
- 1 large onion, chopped
- 4 garlic cloves, finely chopped
- 2 large red bell peppers, seeded and roughly chopped
- 2 large yellow bell peppers, seeded and roughly chopped
- 2 tsp. chopped fresh thyme
- salt and pepper

Method
Bring a large saucepan of water to a boil, and add the rigatoni with a dash of olive oil. Cook for about 10 minutes, stirring occasionally, until tender. Drain and set aside.

Heat the remaining oil in a large skillet. Add the onion, half the garlic, the bell peppers and thyme. Cook over a medium heat for 10–15 minutes, stirring occasionally, until the vegetables are tender and beginning to brown.

Add the pasta shapes to the bell pepper mixture. Stir in the remaining garlic and seasoning. Serve immediately.

Bell Pepper and Pasta Ratatouille

Served with a hot, buttered baked potato, this simple Italian dish is perfectly delicious.

Serves 4–6
- 1 lb. dried wholewheat gnocchi piccoli (small shells)
- dash of olive oil, plus 3 tbsp.
- 2 garlic cloves, crushed
- 1 onion, chopped
- 2 green bell peppers, seeded and cut into chunks
- 14 oz. can chopped tomatoes
- 2 heaped tbsp. tomato paste
- ⅔ cup dry red wine
- 2 tbsp. fresh oregano
- salt and pepper
- fresh oregano sprigs, to garnish

Method
Bring a large saucepan of water to a boil, and add the gnocchi piccoli with a dash of olive oil. Cook for about 10 minutes, stirring occasionally, until tender. Drain and set aside.

Heat the remaining olive oil in a large saucepan and sauté the garlic and onion for about 3 minutes, until softened. Stir in the bell pepper chunks. Cover and cook for about 5 minutes, or until the bell pepper has softened slightly.

Stir the remaining ingredients, except the oregano sprigs, into the bell pepper mixture and bring to simmering point. Reduce the heat, cover, and cook for about 10 minutes, then stir in the gnocchi piccoli. Cook for a further 5 minutes, stirring occasionally. Serve garnished with fresh oregano sprigs.

Left : Bell Pepper and Pasta Ratatouille

127

Pasta with Green Bell Peppers and Pesto

If linguini is unavailable, spaghettini or tagliatelle will work just as well in this dish.

Serves 4

- ◆ 1 lb. fresh linguini (thin, flat strips)
- ◆ dash of olive oil, plus 2 tbsp.
- ◆ 2 garlic cloves, crushed
- ◆ ½ quantity pesto sauce (see p.11)
- ◆ ¼ cup vegetable broth
- ◆ 1 green bell pepper, seeded and very thinly sliced
- ◆ fresh herbs, to garnish

Method

Bring a large saucepan of water to a boil, and add the linguini with a dash of olive oil. Cook for about 4 minutes, stirring occasionally, until tender. Drain and return to the saucepan. Stir in a dash more olive oil and set aside, covered, to keep warm.

Heat the remaining olive oil in a large skillet and sauté the garlic for 1–2 minutes, then stir in the pesto sauce. Add the vegetable broth, stir, and cook for 1 minute, then add the bell pepper slices. Cook for a further 7–10 minutes, stirring occasionally, until the bell pepper has softened. Stir the bell pepper mixture into the linguini and serve, garnished with fresh herbs.

Red Bell Pepper Paste

A paste of broiled red bell peppers has now become a fashionable ingredient, but it has been used in Portugal for many a long year as a flavoring for meat, poultry and fish, grills, and marinades. The garlic cloves can also be broiled, before peeling, if liked. The paste can be kept in a covered glass jar in the refrigerator for 2 weeks.

Makes about 1 cup

- *3 large red bell peppers, seeded and quartered lengthwise*
- *1 tbsp. sea salt*
- *2 garlic cloves*
- *4 tbsp. olive oil*

Method

Stir together the bell peppers and salt; then leave, uncovered, at room temperature for 24 hours.

Preheat the broiler. Rinse the bell peppers well, drain and pat dry. Place, skin side up, on a baking sheet. Broil until the skins are charred and blistered. Leave to cool slightly before peeling off the skins and discarding.

Purée the garlic and bell peppers in a blender, pouring in the oil slowly.

Pasta with Bell Pepper Sauce and Olives

This low-fat bell pepper sauce helps to keep the calories in this Italian dish down. As long as the pasta used is dairy-free, this dish is also suitable for vegans.

Serves 4

- *4½ cups dried rigatoni (short tubes)*
- *dash of olive oil*
- *⅓ cup pitted black olives, roughly chopped*
- *grated Cheddar cheese, to serve*

Bell pepper sauce

- *2 red bell peppers, skinned, seeded, and roughly chopped*
- *4 garlic cloves, peeled*
- *1¼ cups vegetable broth*
- *salt and pepper*

Method

Bring a large saucepan of water to a boil, and add the rigatoni with a dash of olive oil. Cook for about 10 minutes, stirring occasionally, until tender. Drain and return to the saucepan. Set aside.

To make the sauce, place the chopped pepper, garlic and vegetable broth in a food processor or blender, and season with salt and pepper. Purée until smooth.

Stir the bell pepper sauce into the rigatoni with the chopped olives. Serve with grated Cheddar cheese.

Potato and Tomato Pie

Two of Portugal's favorite vegetables are brought together in this simple yet tasty recipe from the Douro. It makes a good supper or lunch dish, or a vegetarian main course, and is a good way of using leftover cooked potatoes.

Serves 4

◆ *about 6 boiled or steamed medium-sized potatoes, thinly sliced*
◆ *Red Bell Pepper Paste (see p.129), for spreading*
◆ *1 bunch of parsley*
◆ *1 garlic clove*
◆ *1 fresh red chili, seeded*
◆ *3 tbsp. virgin olive oil, plus extra for trickling*
◆ *squeeze of lemon juice*
◆ *salt and pepper*
◆ *1¼ lb. well-flavored tomatoes, skinned, seeded and sliced*

Method

Preheat the oven to 400°F.

Lay the potato slices in a well-oiled, shallow baking dish. Spread thinly with Red Bell Pepper Paste.

Chop the parsley, garlic, and chili together and mix with the oil. Add lemon juice and seasoning to taste and spread half over the potatoes. Cover with the tomatoes and spoon over the remaining parsley mixture. Trickle over a little oil and bake for 30–40 minutes. Serve warm, not straight from the oven.

Navy Beans with Tomato Sauce and Onion

This Portuguese recipe is distinguished from other beans in tomato sauce recipes by the addition of a mound of finely chopped raw onion and some chopped cilantro or parsley to each portion as it is served. This really livens up the dish, but it is important to use a mild onion.

Serves 4

- ◆ *8 oz. navy beans, soaked overnight and drained*
- ◆ *3 tbsp. virgin olive oil*
- ◆ *3 garlic cloves, finely chopped*
- ◆ *3 tbsp. chopped parsley*
- ◆ *1 tbsp. chopped mixed thyme and rosemary*
- ◆ *1 bay leaf*
- ◆ *pinch of dried oregano*
- ◆ *¼–½ tsp. crushed red pepper flakes*
- ◆ *1 cup water*
- ◆ *2 large tomatoes, peeled, seeded, and diced*
- ◆ *salt and pepper*
- ◆ *¼ Spanish onion, very finely chopped*
- ◆ *finely chopped cilantro or parsley, to serve*

Method

Put the beans into a saucepan and just cover with water. Boil for 10 minutes and then simmer for about 50 minutes or until the beans are tender.

Heat the oil, garlic, herbs, and crushed red pepper gently for 4 minutes. Add the water, bring to a boil, then cover and simmer for 5 minutes. Stir in the tomatoes, cover again and simmer for 4 minutes.

Drain the beans and stir into the tomato mixture gently. Season and simmer for 4–5 minutes.

Ladle the beans and sauce into four warmed soup plates and put a small mound of onion and some cilantro or parsley in the center of each.

Lentils and Rice

Biblical anthropologists believe that Esau's "mess of pottage," as recorded in the Book of Genesis, was composed of rice and lentils – a version of the Lebanese dish eaten today. Every family has its special way of making this staple, varying the proportions and/or the spicing. Cinnamon is not traditional, but it is sometimes added as it is believe to increase sexual prowess and give strength to the ill.

Serves 6–8

- *1 cup brown lentils, washed and picked over*
- *5 tbsp. olive oil*
- *4 large onions, sliced*
- *1⅓ cups long-grain rice, washed*
- *salt and pepper*
- *¼ tsp. cinnamon (optional)*

Method

Bring a large saucepan of water to a boil, add the lentils, cover and simmer for about 25–30 minutes, until just soft.

Meanwhile, heat the olive oil in a heatproof casserole with a cover, and stir in the sliced onions. Cook over medium-low heat until the onions are limp and just beginning to color. Remove half of them with a slotted spoon and set aside. Cook the remainder, being careful not to let them burn, until brown and glazed. Remove from the heat and transfer the onions to a bowl.

Drain the cooked lentils reserving the liquid. Return the lightly cooked onions to the casserole and stir in the rice. Cook until the rice is just transparent, then stir in the drained lentils, salt and pepper to taste, the cinnamon, if desired, and enough of the cooking liquid to cover well. Cook the "pottage," covered, over low heat until the rice has absorbed all the water. If the rice and lentils are not tender yet, add a little more liquid. Stir in the caramelized onions and serve immediately.

Lentils and Burghul

This is a Lebanese alternative to Lentils and Rice (above) and, like that dish, serves as a staple of the poor. It makes a substantial dish with a poached or fried egg on top of each serving. (Cooked garbanzo beans can be substituted for the cooked lentils.)

Serves 6

- *5 tbsp. olive oil*
- *3 onions, thinly sliced*
- *1 cup brown lentils, washed and picked over*
- *1½ cups medium-ground burghul*
- *salt and pepper*
- *cayenne pepper*

Method

Heat the oil in a skillet. Fry the onions until they are limp and lightly colored – about 8–10 minutes. Remove about a third of the onions with a slotted spoon and reserve; continue to cook the remaining onions until they are browned. Reserve them.

In a heatproof casserole, cook the lentils in water to cover for about 25 minutes or until just tender. (Add more water during cooking, if necessary, but do not make it too soupy.) Add the burghul, the light-colored onions, salt, pepper and cayenne to taste. Stir to combine, cover, and let the burghul soak up the remaining moisture (add a bit more, if necessary) for about 10–12 minutes. Stir in the browned onions and serve immediately.

Potatoes with Garbanzo Beans

This is another popular, filling dish from the
Lebanon which can also do service as a main
course. If served as a vegetarian main course,
I lb. fresh spinach can be stirred into the
potatoes and garbanzo beans in the last
5 minutes of cooking and left to wilt.

Serves 6

- ½ cup olive oil
- 1 large onion, chopped
- 12 oz. small red potatoes, washed and cut into
  small pieces
- 2 garlic cloves, finely chopped
- 2½ cups cooked and drained garbanzo beans
- 5 medium tomatoes, peeled, seeded, and
  chopped
- cayenne pepper
- ½ tsp. coriander seeds
- salt and pepper
- 1 cup finely chopped fresh parsley

Method

Heat the olive oil in a heatproof casserole
with a cover. Add the onion and cook until
it is lightly colored and limp. Add the
chopped potatoes and the garlic, and cook,
stirring, over low heat for 3–4 minutes.
Stir in the garbanzo beans, the tomatoes,
cayenne pepper to taste and the
coriander seeds.

Cover and simmer for 20 minutes, or until
the potatoes are soft. Season to taste and stir
in the chopped parsley before serving.

This dish can also be cooled, chilled
overnight and served cold.

Braised Lentils

A Portuguese dish that is filling and economical – the theory is that if a large, steaming bowl of these well-flavored lentils accompanies a meat dish, the amount of meat eaten will be reduced. The lentils are so good that the theory is always accurate.

Serves 4
- *2 tbsp. olive oil*
- *1 onion, finely chopped*
- *1 plump garlic clove, crushed*
- *1 leek, chopped*
- *1 carrot, chopped*
- *1 potato, chopped*
- *1 large tomato, peeled and chopped*
- *generous 1 cup brown lentils*
- *2½ cups veal, chicken, or vegetable stock*
- *1 bouquet garni*
- *2 anchovy fillets, chopped*
- *2 tsp. wine vinegar*
- *salt and pepper*

Method

Heat the oil in a saucepan, add the onion and cook until softened and lightly colored. Stir in the garlic, leek, carrot, and potato, and cook for 4–5 minutes. Stir in the tomato, followed by the lentils a minute or so later.

When everything is mixed together, add the stock and bouquet garni, bring to a boil and simmer for 30–40 minutes until the lentils and vegetables are tender.

Discard the bouquet garni. Purée about one-third of the lentil mixture with the anchovy fillets and vinegar in a blender. Return to the pan, reheat and season.

Brown Beans with Herbs

These small brown beans are members of the fava family, of a specific type native to Egypt and the Levant. They are served with egg on top for breakfast, mashed into a purée with extra oil and lemon juice for *mezze*, or prepared as in this recipe, for a main course with meats, or for a side dish. There are restaurants in the Middle East – Egypt especially – that specialize in *ful* dishes.

Serves 4–6

- *1½ cups ful medames (brown beans), washed, picked over and soaked for 24 hours in a cool place*
- *5 tbsp. olive oil*
- *juice of 1 lemon*
- *3 garlic cloves, crushed*
- *salt and pepper*
- *1 tsp. cumin*
- *3 tbsp. finely chopped cilantro*
- *extra olive oil and lemon wedges (optional)*

Method

Drain and rinse the beans. Bring a large saucepan – with just less than twice the volume of water to beans – to the boil and add the beans. Cover, bring to a boil again, reduce the heat and simmer for about 2½ hours, or until the beans are tender. Skim the top of the cooking liquid at the beginning to remove any scum. By the end of cooking, the water should have reduced and thickened. If the beans are still too soupy, strain off some of the liquid.

Stir in the oil, lemon juice, garlic, salt and pepper, cumin and cilantro. Transfer the beans to a serving bowl and offer hot, or allow to cool and serve cold, with extra olive oil and lemon wedges.

Fava Beans with Cilantro

A liberal amount of chopped cilantro and some chopped tomato stirred into the beans just before serving make this Portuguese recipe a particularly interesting and memorable way of serving fava beans.

Serves 4

- ◆ *2 oz. piece of bacon, cut into strips*
- ◆ *1 onion, finely chopped*
- ◆ *1 lb. shelled fresh or thawed frozen fava beans*
- ◆ *salt and pepper*
- ◆ *2 tomatoes, peeled, seeded, and chopped*
- ◆ *¾ cup chopped cilantro*

Method

Cook the bacon in a heavy saucepan until the fat runs. Stir in the onion and cook until softened. Add the beans, barely cover with water and simmer until they are tender, 6–15 minutes depending on the age of the beans; or cook according to the directions on the package if using frozen beans.

Strain the beans and return to the pan. Stir in the seasoning and tomatoes, cover and heat gently, shaking the pan occasionally, for a few minutes to warm the tomatoes. Stir in the cilantro and serve.

Tomato and Pasta Salad

Orecchiette are small, ear-shaped pasta. If they are not available, gnocchi pasta shapes (dumplings) will work just as well.

Serves 6–8
- 1¼ lb. fresh orecchiette (ears)
- dash of olive oil
- 1 lb. red and yellow tomatoes, chopped
- 6-in. piece cucumber, chopped
- 6 oz. Feta cheese, chopped
- 5 tbsp. chopped cilantro
- 2 tbsp. chopped fresh basil

Dressing
- 1 tbsp. white wine vinegar
- 4 tbsp. olive oil
- 2 garlic cloves, crushed
- salt and pepper

Garnish
- cherry tomatoes
- fresh cilantro sprigs

Method
Bring a large saucepan of water to a boil, and add the orecchiette with a dash of olive oil. Cook for about 5 minutes, stirring occasionally, until tender. Drain and rinse under cold running water. Drain again, and set aside.

Place the orecchiette in a large mixing bowl, and add the remaining salad ingredients. Mix to combine.

To make the dressing, place all the ingredients in a screw-top jar and shake well. Pour the dressing over the salad, and toss to coat. Serve garnished with cherry tomatoes and cilantro sprigs.

Grilled Tomato Salad with Red Bell Peppers

The tomatoes and peppers can be charred over a barbecue, as is often done in the Algarve, Portugal, from where this salad comes. Two or three unpeeled garlic cloves can also be grilled, then either crushed and used in the dressing, or sliced and mixed with the tomatoes and peppers.

Serves 4
- *1¼ lb. firm, but ripe, well-flavored tomatoes*
- *2 red bell peppers*
- *6 tbsp. olive oil*
- *1½ tbsp. mild red wine vinegar*
- *1 garlic clove, crushed*
- *salt and pepper*
- *chopped cilantro or parsley, to serve*

Method
Preheat the barbecue or broiler.

Grill the tomatoes and bell peppers, turning frequently, until evenly charred and blistered. Leave until cool enough to handle and then peel them.

Slice the tomatoes. Cut the bell peppers in half and discard the cores and seeds; then slice the flesh.

Mix together the tomatoes and bell peppers. Whisk together the oil, vinegar, garlic, and seasoning, pour over the vegetables and leave for about 1 hour.

Serve sprinkled with cilantro or parsley.

Tomato Rice

This is one of the most popular of the many Portuguese rice dishes. Much of its character comes from the well-flavored, locally grown tomatoes, so choose them carefully; many stores are now selling varieties that have been grown specifically for their flavor. If the rice is still soggy at the end of cooking, it is described as *malandrinho* (naughty). Serve the rice with roast, broiled or fried meat, poultry and fish, fish cakes, and omelets.

Serves 4
- *2 tbsp. olive oil*
- *1 large onion, finely chopped*
- *1 garlic clove, finely chopped*
- *2 ripe, well-flavored tomatoes, skinned, seeded and finely chopped*
- *generous 1 cup long-grain rice*
- *boiling water*
- *2 tbsp. chopped parsley*
- *salt and pepper*

Method
Heat the oil in a saucepan, add the onion and garlic, and fry until softened but not brown.

Stir in the tomatoes and cook for a further 5 minutes or so before adding the rice. Stir to coat with the vegetables; then add boiling water to 2½ times the volume of the rice. Bring to a boil, cover and cook over a low heat until the rice is tender and all the liquid has been absorbed. Stir in the parsley and seasoning to taste.

Tortellini, Bell Peppers, and Pine Nut Salad

Red bell peppers can be used instead of chili peppers, if you prefer. For best results, allow the salad to chill for at least an hour before serving.

Serves 4–6

- ◆ *scant ¼ lb. fresh tortellini*
- ◆ *dash of olive oil*
- ◆ *1 onion, very finely sliced*
- ◆ *1 green bell pepper, seeded and very finely diced*
- ◆ *⅔ cup toasted pine nuts*
- ◆ *1 red chili pepper, seeded and sliced (optional)*
- ◆ *4-in. piece of cucumber, very thinly sliced*
- ◆ *1 orange, peeled and very thinly sliced*

Dressing

- ◆ *4 tbsp. olive oil*
- ◆ *2 tbsp. sweet soy sauce*
- ◆ *2 tbsp. vinegar*
- ◆ *salt and pepper*

Method

Bring a large saucepan of water to a boil, and add the tortellini with a dash of olive oil. Cook for about 4 minutes, stirring occasionally, until tender. Drain and rinse under cold running water. Drain again and set aside.

Place the tortellini in a large mixing bowl and add the remaining salad ingredients. Toss together lightly.

To make the salad dressing, place the ingredients in a screw-top jar and shake well to combine. Pour the dressing over the salad, toss, and serve.

Minty Bell Pepper Salad

Serve this for a summer lunch, or a picnic.

Serves 4

- ◆ 3¼ cups dried macaroni
- ◆ dash of olive oil, plus extra for drizzling
- ◆ 1 yellow bell pepper, seeded and chopped
- ◆ 1 green bell pepper, seeded and chopped
- ◆ 14 oz. can artichoke hearts, drained and quartered
- ◆ 6-in. piece of cucumber, sliced
- ◆ handful of mint leaves
- ◆ salt and pepper
- ◆ 1⅓ cups freshly grated Parmesan cheese

Method

Bring a large saucepan of water to a boil, and add the macaroni with a dash of olive oil. Cook for about 10 minutes, stirring occasionally, until tender. Drain, and rinse under cold running water. Drain again, then place in a large mixing bowl.

Add the remaining ingredients to the pasta and mix well to combine. Drizzle some olive oil over the salad, then serve.

Tomato and Cheese Salad

This semi-hard cheese has a slight tang.

Serves 4

- 1¼ lb. well-flavored tomatoes, sliced
- 4 oz. sheep's cheese, coarsely chopped or sliced
- chopped cilantro

To serve

- olive oil
- 2 lemons, halved
- salt and pepper

Method

Arrange the tomato slices in a shallow bowl and scatter the cheese on top. Sprinkle with chopped cilantro and serve with the oil, lemon halves, and seasoning for each person to add their own, in that order.

CHAPTER 6

CAKES AND DESSERTS

....

You don't have to be an expert cook to produce the sort of dessert that typically finishes a Mediterranean meal. Pastries, fruit and milky desserts are treated with the unfussy hand that characterizes this cuisine, and the cakes place more importance on yummy tastes and textures than elaborate decoration.

Apricot Tart

All the elements of this Portuguese tart complement each other perfectly – the lush, soft filling, topped by juicy sweet apricots held in an almond-flavored pastry. The best cheese to use is ricotta, or failing that, medium- or full-fat curd cheese.

Serves 6–8
- *1¼ cups all-purpose flour*
- *5 tbsp. superfine sugar*
- *finely grated zest and juice of 1 orange*
- *1 egg yolk*
- *¼ tsp. vanilla extract*
- *½ cup plus 2 tbsp. unsalted butter, diced*

Filling
- *1 lb. ricotta or curd cheese*
- *1 cup superfine sugar*
- *4 eggs*
- *6 tbsp. heavy cream*
- *few drops of almond extract*

Topping
- *1 lb. apricots*
- *2 tbsp. apricot jam*

Method
Stir the flour, sugar and half the orange zest together in a bowl. Make a well in the center and add the egg yolk, vanilla extract, and butter. Using your fingertips, mix together to make a smooth dough, adding 1–2

teaspoons orange juice. Cover and chill.

Preheat the oven to 400°F. Roll out half the dough and use to line the bottom of a buttered 9-inch loose-bottomed, spring-form cake pan. Bake for 15 minutes and then leave to cool.

Meanwhile, make the filling. Beat the cheese with the sugar and remaining orange zest; then gradually beat in the eggs. Stir in the cream and almond extract.

Roll out the remaining pastry and use to line the sides of the cake pan, pressing the bottom edge on to the partly cooked base. Pour in the filling and bake for 15 minutes; then lower the temperature to 325°F and bake for 20 minutes until just set.

Plunge the apricots into boiling water, leave for a few seconds, then lift out and remove the skin. Halve the fruit and remove the pits. Arrange the apricots over the filling and bake for 10 minutes.

Leave to cool in the pan before transferring to a serving dish. Heat the apricot jam and remaining orange juice. Brush over the apricots.

Marmalade Crêpes

A tasty Greek dessert in which the crêpes can be made well ahead and stacked on a plate. Cover with aluminum foil and reheat in a low oven for about 15 minutes before finishing with the marmalade and cinnamon sugar to serve.

Makes about 24

- 2 eggs, *beaten*
- 1 tbsp. *superfine sugar*
- *few drops of vanilla extract*
- 2½ cups milk
- 2 cups all-purpose flour, *sifted*
- *butter for greasing*
- *marmalade*
- *ground cinnamon mixed with superfine sugar*

Method

Place the eggs and sugar in a medium-sized bowl and beat, preferably with an electric mixer, until thick, pale and frothy. Beat in the vanilla extract and then the milk, a little at a time, until well combined.

Beat the sifted flour into the egg mixture, a little at a time, beating well after each addition to prevent any lumps from forming.

Melt a little butter in a small crêpe pan or skillet and add about 2 tablespoons of the batter, swirling it around to cover the base of the pan evenly. Cook over high heat for a few seconds, or until golden underneath, then flip over with a spatula and cook for a further few seconds until golden.

Tip the cooked crêpe onto a plate and continue with the remaining batter, melting a little extra butter in the pan if necessary. Pile up the cooked crêpes, interleaving them with sheets of waxed paper to prevent them sticking together.

To serve, spread a little marmalade over each crêpe and roll up thinly. Arrange the rolled crêpes on a warm serving plate, overlapping and piling them up where necessary. Sprinkle with the cinnamon-sugar mixture while still warm.

Yogurt and Orange Mousse Cake

This is a modern dessert from Lebanon with the flavors and spirit of the old Levant married to the health concerns of the new. It is very simple to make.

Serves 6

- *3 large eggs, separated*
- *½ cup milk*
- *1 cup Greek-style yogurt*
- *½ tsp. grated orange zest*
- *4 tbsp. fresh orange juice*
- *generous 1 cup sugar*
- *2 tbsp. flour*
- *1 tsp. vanilla extract*
- *sweetened fruit yogurt (optional)*

Method

Preheat the oven to 350°F. In a bowl, with an electric mixer, beat the separated egg yolks until thickened and pale. Add the milk and yogurt, grated zest and orange juice, then beat in three-quarters of the sugar, flour and vanilla until the mixture is smooth.

In a large bowl beat the egg whites on medium speed until they are foamy. Turn the speed up to high, and beat in the remaining sugar until stiff peaks form.

Gently fold the yolk mixture into the whites until all is combined. Pour the batter into a 9-inch square cake pan.

Place the pan in a larger container and pour in boiling water until it comes halfway up the outer sides of the cake pan. Bake the cake in the oven for about 30 minutes or until it is golden. Serve with sweetened fruit yogurt, if desired.

Phyllo Custard Pie

A Greek classic – a similar idea to Baklava (see p.156), and just as sweet and irresistible.

Makes about 24
- ◆ *1 lb. phyllo pastry dough*
- ◆ *½ cup unsalted butter, melted*
- ◆ *2 tsp. lemon juice*

Syrup
- ◆ *2¼ cups superfine sugar*
- ◆ *1¼ cups water*
- ◆ *1 cinnamon stick*
- ◆ *few whole cloves*
- ◆ *1 tbsp. brandy*
- ◆ *1 tbsp. freshly squeezed orange juice*

Filling
- ◆ *heaped 1 cup superfine sugar*
- ◆ *⅓ cup fine semolina*
- ◆ *6¼ cups milk*
- ◆ *1 tbsp. brandy*
- ◆ *3 eggs*
- ◆ *finely grated zest of ½ orange*

Method

To make the syrup, place the sugar and water in a large saucepan and stir over a low heat until all the sugar has dissolved. Add the cinnamon stick and cloves and bring to a boil. Boil rapidly for 10–12 minutes. Remove from the heat and stir in the remaining syrup ingredients. Set aside to cool. Remove the cinnamon and cloves.

Preheat the oven to 350°F. Lightly butter a 12 × 9 × 3-inch roasting pan.

To make the filling, place the sugar and semolina in a large saucepan. Gradually stir in the milk and heat gently, stirring continuously, until the mixture thickens, making sure no lumps appear. Stir in the brandy and remove from the heat.

Place the eggs in a mixing bowl and beat until pale and frothy. Add the semolina mixture and beat again until evenly combined. Add the orange zest. Allow to cool down slightly.

Layer about half of the phyllo pastry dough in the base of the prepared pan, brushing each sheet evenly with melted butter before layering the next. Spoon in the filling mixture and spread evenly over the base. Top with the remaining sheets of phyllo pastry dough, brushing each one with the melted butter.

Using a sharp knife, score the top layers of the phyllo pastry dough, dividing the pie into 2-inch diamonds or squares. Bake for 45 minutes, or until crisp and golden on top and the filling is set. Remove from the oven and stand the pan on a wire rack. Pour the syrup evenly over the top and leave to stand for at least 4 hours, but preferably overnight. Serve cut into small pieces.

Caramel Custard

Caramel custard is so widely and so frequently eaten in Portugal that it has been nicknamed "365," indicating the number of days in the year on which most restaurants serve it. Typically, Portuguese caramel custard is rich in egg yolks.

Serves 4
◆ 6 tbsp. sugar
◆ 4 tbsp. water
◆ 2 cups hot milk
◆ 3 eggs, separated
◆ 5 large egg yolks

Method
Preheat the oven to 350°F. Place four dariole molds or custard cups in a baking pan.

Heat the sugar and water gently in a small heavy-based saucepan until the sugar has dissolved; then boil rapidly until golden-brown. Remove from the heat and pour in the milk very slowly and carefully. Stir to dissolve the caramel completely. Beat the egg yolks lightly and stir in the caramel-flavored milk.

Strain the mixture into the molds and pour boiling water into the baking pan. Bake for 20–25 minutes until just set in the center. Remove the dishes from the baking pan and leave to cool. Cover and chill lightly.

Nun's Belly

In Portugal, as in many other countries, nuns made and often sold sweetmeats, cakes, cookies, and preserves.

Serves 4
◆ 1 cup sugar
◆ ¾ cup water
◆ 2 tbsp. unsalted butter, diced
◆ 4 cups fresh white bread crumbs
◆ 8 egg yolks, beaten

Decoration
◆ ground cinnamon
◆ toasted slivered almonds

Method
Heat the sugar in the water gently, stirring occasionally, until the sugar has dissolved: then boil to a fairly thick syrup. Remove from the heat, stir in the butter until it has melted and then mix in the bread crumbs. Put the saucepan over a very low heat and stir in the egg yolks gradually. Cook, stirring constantly, until thickened; do not allow the mixture to boil. Transfer to a serving dish and sprinkle with ground cinnamon and toasted almonds.

Honey and Orange Figs

A simple, refreshing fruit dessert from Portugal.

Serves 4

- ◆ *2 tbsp. clear honey*
- ◆ *1 tbsp. lemon juice*
- ◆ *4 tbsp. orange juice*
- ◆ *4 ripe figs, sliced into rings*
- ◆ *2 oranges, peeled and segmented*
- ◆ *4 mint sprigs*

Method

Stir the honey into the fruit juices until it has dissolved. Put the fruit into a dish, pour over the honey mixture and stir together lightly. Cover and chill for at least 1 hour.

Stir gently before dividing between 4 chilled dishes. Decorate each serving with a sprig of mint.

Peaches in Red Wine

During the peach-growing season, large bowls of these peaches are available at the Herdade de Zambujal, a huge peach-growing estate on the Costa Azul in Portugal.

Serves 6
- ◆ *6 peaches*
- ◆ *1 cinnamon stick*
- ◆ *½–¾ bottle of red wine*
- ◆ *½ cup superfine sugar*
- ◆ *ground cinnamon, to serve*

Method
Preheat the oven to 350°F. Pour boiling water over the peaches and leave for about 30–60 seconds; then remove with a slotted spoon and slip off the skins. If the skins are stubborn, return the peaches briefly to the water.

Put the peaches into a baking dish which they just fit, tuck the cinnamon stick in between them and pour over enough wine to cover them. Sprinkle over the sugar and bake for 40–50 minutes until the peaches are tender.

Remove from the oven, discard the cinnamon stick, turn the peaches over and leave to cool in the wine, turning once or twice more. Serve dusted lightly with ground cinnamon.

Mixed Fruit Compote

The perfect accompaniment to this delicious Greek dessert is lashings of thick Greek yogurt.

Serves 8–10
- *12 oz. pears*
- *12 oz. apples*
- *12 oz. peaches*
- *12 oz. apricots*
- *2 tbsp. lemon juice*
- *3½ cups superfine sugar*
- *2 cinnamon sticks*
- *3¾ cups water*
- *3–4 whole cloves*
- *strip of lemon zest*

Method
To prepare the fruit for the compote, peel, core and quarter the pears and apples. Wash the peaches and apricots, and remove the stones. Cut the peaches into quarters and apricots in half.

Place the pear and apple quarters in a large, heavy-based saucepan with the lemon juice, sugar, cinnamon sticks, water, cloves and lemon zest. Gently bring to a boil and simmer for 5 minutes.

Add the peaches and cook for a further 5 minutes, then add the apricot halves and continue to cook for 3–5 minutes or until softened. Using a slotted spoon, transfer the fruit to a serving bowl, cover and set aside.

Return the syrup to a boil and continue to boil rapidly for about 10 minutes, or until reduced slightly and thickened. Remove the cinnamon sticks, cloves and lemon zest. Allow the syrup to cool, then pour over the fruit. Serve at room temperature or chilled.

Egg Cakes in Syrup

The exact translation of the Portuguese title for this dish is "Angels' Breasts." It is another of the sweet, rich egg dishes so beloved by the Portuguese.

Serves 4–6
- *butter*
- *4 large egg yolks*
- *1 large egg white*
- *1 cup sugar*
- *½ cup water*
- *few drops of vanilla or almond extract*

Method
Preheat the oven to 350°F. Butter 12 × 2-inch muffin pans, dariole molds or custard cups generously.
Whisk the egg yolks until very thick and pale. With a clean whisk, whisk the egg white until stiff but not dry: then stir 3 spoonfuls into the egg yolks. Fold in the remaining egg white gently. Divide between the pans or molds and stand in a roasting pan. Pour in sufficient boiling water to come halfway up the sides of the pans or dishes and bake for 15–20 minutes until set.

Meanwhile, heat the sugar in the water gently, stirring until dissolved; then boil until it is a thick syrup. Add a few drops of vanilla or almond extract.

Leave the cooked cakes to cool in the pans or dishes for a few minutes before unmolding. Dip them into the syrup and then put them into a large, shallow serving plate or bowl. Pour over the remaining syrup and chill well.

Chocolate Refrigerator Torte

From Greece, a deliciously rich chocolate dessert which can be made several days ahead.

Serves 10–12

- 2⅔ cups coarse graham cracker crumbs
- ½ cup milk
- 2 tbsp. brandy
- 1 cup butter, softened
- heaped 1 cup superfine sugar
- 3 eggs, separated
- 2 tsp. vanilla extract
- 4 tbsp. cocoa powder
- ¾ cup blanched almonds, toasted and roughly chopped
- vegetable oil for greasing

Method

Place the cracker crumbs in a large mixing bowl. Pour the milk and brandy over them and allow to soak until the liquid has been absorbed.Place the butter and sugar in a medium-sized bowl and beat until well blended and creamy. Beat in the egg yolks, then add the vanilla extract, cocoa powder and chopped nuts.

Beat the egg whites in a clean, dry bowl and fold into the chocolate mixture. Stir in the soaked cracker crumbs. Lightly grease a 5-cup bread pan, line with waxed paper and pour in the chocolate mixture. Spread evenly in the pan and freeze for about 4 hours, or until solid. Remove from the freezer about 30 minutes before serving and keep chilled in the refrigerator. Turn out onto a serving plate and cut into thin slices to serve.

Baklava

Method

Preheat the oven to 325°F. Butter a 12 × 9 × 3-inch roasting pan. Trim the sheets of phyllo pastry dough to fit inside the pan and discard the trimmings.

Place the first sheet of phyllo dough in the base of the prepared pan and brush evenly with melted butter. Lay another sheet of phyllo on top and brush again with the melted butter. Repeat this process until you have 12 sheets of phyllo pastry dough layered on the bottom of the pan. Cover the remaining phyllo pastry dough with a slightly damp cloth to prevent it from drying out while you work.

To make the filling, place the honey in a medium-sized bowl. Add the lemon juice and stir until combined. Stir in the sugar, ground cinnamon, lemon zest and nuts. Spread half of the filling mixture over the phyllo in the base of the pan.

Layer another three sheets of phyllo pastry dough on top of the filling, brushing each sheet with melted butter. Spread the remaining filling mixture over the phyllo and cover with the remaining sheets of phyllo, brushing each sheet with melted butter. Brush the top with any remaining butter and score into 2-inch diamond shapes. Bake for about 1 hour, or until crisp and golden. Remove to a wire rack.

To make the syrup, place all the ingredients together in a medium-sized saucepan and heat gently until the sugar has dissolved completely. Increase the heat and boil rapidly for about 10 minutes, without stirring. Set aside to cool. Discard the cinnamon stick and lemon zest and pour the syrup evenly over the pastry. Ideally, the baklava should stand at room temperature overnight before it is cut into diamond-shaped pieces.

Makes about 24

- ¾ cup unsalted butter, melted
- 1 lb. phyllo pastry, thawed if frozen

Filling

- 4 tbsp. clear honey
- 2 tbsp. lemon juice
- ¼ cup superfine sugar
- 2 tsp. ground cinnamon
- 1 tsp. finely grated lemon zest
- 1⅓ cups blanched almonds, roughly chopped
- 1⅓ cups shelled walnuts, roughly chopped

Syrup

- 1¾ cups superfine sugar
- 5 tbsp. clear honey
- 2½ cups water
- 1 cinnamon stick
- strip of lemon zest

Sweet Milk Clouds

This is a favorite dessert throughout Portugal, especially in restaurants.

Serves 4
- 1 vanilla bean
- 2 cups milk
- 4 eggs, separated
- generous ½ cup sugar

Method

Put the vanilla bean and milk in a heavy-based, preferably non-stick, saucepan and bring to a boil slowly. Remove from the heat, cover and leave for 20 minutes.

Whisk the egg yolks with ½ cup of the sugar until thick. Remove the vanilla bean from the milk and bring the milk back to a boil. Stir into the egg yolk mixture slowly and return to the pan. Heat very gently, stirring constantly, until thickened; do not allow it to boil.

Leave to cool, stirring occasionally, and then strain into a shallow serving bowl or individual bowls. Cover and chill.

Whisk the egg whites until stiff and whisk in the remaining sugar gradually.

Heat a wide, shallow pan of water to simmering point. Drop large spoonfuls of egg white on to the water, spacing them slightly apart, and poach gently for about 4 minutes, turning them after 2 minutes. Lift out with a slotted spoon and drain on several thicknesses of paper towels.

Float the "clouds" on the custard and serve.

Left : Baklava

INDEX